ON THE WAY

Towards an Integrated Approach to Christian Initiation

GS Misc 444

ON THE WAY

Towards an Integrated Approach to Christian Initiation

CHURCH HOUSE PUBLISHING
Church House, Great Smith Street, London SW1P 3NZ

ISBN 0 7151 3761 1

Published 1995 for the General Synod of the Church of England by Church House Publishing

Extracts from John Finney, *Finding Faith Today* (Bible Society/Churches Together in England, 1992); John Finney, *Church on the Move* (DLT, 1992); *Walk in Newness of Life: The Findings of the International Anglican Liturgical Consultation, Toronto, 1991* (Anglican Book Centre, 1993); Steve Croft, *Growing New Christians* (Marshall Pickering, 1993) are reproduced with thanks.

Printed in England by Rapier Press Ltd.

CONTENTS

Foreword by the Chairman of the House of Bishops

In July 1991 the General Synod asked the House of Bishops, in consultation with others, to prepare a paper 'on patterns of nurture in the faith, including the Catechumenate'.

This Report is the work of a Group appointed by the House, under the Chairmanship of the Bishop of St Edmundsbury and Ipswich, to prepare a response to the General Synod's request. The House is grateful to the Group for the Report which is a helpful further contribution to continuing debate within the Church on Christian Initiation issues.

In this Decade of Evangelism the welcome and nurture of new Christians is one of the most important tasks that faces the Christian community. We shall, as a House, be considering this Report (and responses to it) with the greatest care over the coming months. We hope too that it will be widely considered within the Church.

On behalf of the House
+ George Cantuar
Chairman

October 1994

PREFACE

Can the Church better help people into a real, intelligent, shared and living belief within the community of faith – and what means can be engaged to further this?

This Report, in response to the call of the General Synod in July 1991 and to a subsequent request by the House of Bishops, seeks to suggest a possible route towards an integrated response to this question. Setting the scene, it describes a variety of stories of individual journeys of faith. Recognising and affirming the multiplicity of approaches and resources which are already to be found, it studies the catechumenate as an approach to Christian initiation, and sees in it a hopeful and positive framework on which a comprehensive way forward could be based.

The Group which undertook most of the work had representatives on it from the Board of Mission, the Board of Education and the Liturgical Commission:

Mrs Sarah James
The Bishop of Pontefract
The Revd Sue Cummings
The Bishop of Middleton
The Bishop of Salisbury
The Revd Michael Vasey

My thanks go to all its members, three of whom have become bishops during the course of our deliberations! My particular thanks go to the Reverend Michael Vasey who, on our behalf, has devoted much time and skill towards its writing and crafting and to St John's College, Durham for making his time available.

I believe that the report will make a major contribution both to the debate and to the development of a more integrated approach to Christian initiation in the Church of England.

October 1994

+ John St Edmundsbury and Ipswich
Chairman of the Group

SUMMARY

What is this report about? It is a detailed study of Christian initiation and in particular of the plan of the catechumenate.

This summary sets out some of the main suggestions made, and identifies these by reference to the relevant paragraph numbers in the report. This will assist readers to track down the proposals and the reasoning behind them.

The Importance of Christian Initiation

Parishes and congregations need to have a clear and developing grasp of their approach to initiation. This implies the involvement of the PCC and wider Church fellowship and not simply an initiative by the clergy. Furthermore such parish policies and approaches must have regard for those particular concerns which are embodied in the bishop's oversight of initiation. This means that each parish would need to identify and own its approach for the welcome and formation of new believers, and these approaches should be worked out in appropriate dialogue with the bishop and should cover:

the welcome, formation and sacramental initiation of adult enquirers;

an appropriate pattern for responding to requests by non-church going parents for their children's baptism;

the appropriate time for admission to communion of children baptised in infancy;

provision (where appropriate) marking the entry into adulthood of young people growing up within the church (paragraph 8.2).

Three patterns now co-exist in the Church of England:

the Reformation tradition of confirmation, as simultaneously the gateway to communion and to Christian adulthood;

confirmation of younger children as their entry to communion, recognising that their entry into Christian adulthood will follow at a later stage;

the admission of the baptised to communion, with confirmation coming later as a gateway to Christian adulthood (paragraph 5.56).

We hope that a wider appreciation of an integrated approach to the initiation and formation of Christians, such as is modelled in catechumenate approaches, may lead to a greater understanding and unity between different approaches in the Church of England. The issues which need to be addressed include whether:

> (i) parishes should be designated according to which of the initiation patterns they are following;

> (ii) candidates from different options should be confirmed at different services;

> (iii) children admitted to communion under the third pattern should be issued with a diocesan certificate that makes it clear that they are communicants (paragraph 5.57).

The gospel is about freedom in Christ, a concept itself that needs to be affirmed and explored during initial formation. A catechetical process that fails to respect the conscience of individuals or attempts an over-rigid moral formation risks damaging the individual (paragraph 4.68.iii).

The Nature of the Catechumenate

The Group sees the catechumenate as a positive model for Christian initiation. It welcomes the opportunity to attempt to provide an integrated overview of this vital part of the life of the Church (paragraph 1.7).

We follow the usage recommended in the Toronto statement, limiting 'catechumen' and 'catechumenate' to the unbaptised and using the term 'catechumenal process' for any process that follows the approach set out above (paragraph 3.5).

We do not propose a single elaborate series of stages and rites as set out in the Roman Catholic *Rite of Christian Initiation of Adults*. . . . The better way seems to be to affirm what is good in present practice, to recognise that the Church of England is in a learning process, and to identify ways in which present practice might be improved (paragraph 6.2).

We suggest that the term 'catechumen' should not be used in any official liturgical provision but that . . . the term 'enquirer' could be adopted (paragraph 3.33).

The Church of England should give formal recognition to the status of 'enquirer'. An enquirer would be a person, baptised or unbaptised, who, with the prayers and support of the Church, enters into a public exploration of the Christian way (paragraph 6.3.i).

The Process of Learning

The baptismal practice of a Church needs to be judged in part by the answer it would give to an unchurched parent who said, 'This is who we are; this is our starting point. How will you meet and help us?' (paragraph 5.7).

A personal Rule of Life is a helpful discipline which individuals should be helped to work out and adopt (paragraph 6.11.4).

A 'knapsack' of liturgical and devotional material for individual use needs to be identified. The purpose of such a knapsack would be to provide the individual with a core of devotional material which could inform his or her private prayer, be available in time of need, and provide a link between personal devotion and the public prayer of the Church (paragraph 6.11.5).

We recommend that the Lord's Prayer, the Apostles' Creed, Jesus' summary of the law, and the Beatitudes be available as texts which could be taken as a liturgical focus for formation (paragraph 3.48).

Clergy cannot give the time and personal attention that proper involvement with Christian formation requires. Lay people are in a position to stand alongside those coming to faith, to sympathise with them, and to journey with them. Lay people should also play a part in the rites that mark and affirm the journey of faith.

'The basic question is, "What are sufficient iron rations for a Christian?" The answer may well be regular reception of the eucharist . . . private prayer . . . an accepting group. All else is luxury. The Church should provide these but little else – except appropriate support to people in their work/home environment and helping others to find faith'.

Christian initiation is not about socialising people into the rules and practice of a club. It involves encounter with the dynamic presence and mission of the living God (paragraph 8.4).

A new Catechism should be prepared (paragraph 6.11.6).

3

Liturgical Provision

We believe that the Church of England should make available flexible rites for those approaching baptism or the renewal of their baptismal commitment . . . (paragraph 3.40).

The Church of England should make available additional forms of prayer that could be used before and after baptism, confirmation, reaffirmation of faith, or reception into communion. The purpose of these forms would be to enable a local congregation to journey with candidates for one or other of these rites (paragraph 6.3.ii).

The Liturgical Commission may consider providing:

1. A rite of welcome for an enquirer.

2. Prayers for those exploring the Way.

3. Rites to precede and follow public celebrations of baptism, confirmation, reaffirmation or reception. . . . These rites might consist of:

    a. a rite of call and response in which enquirers or others are accepted as candidates for baptism, confirmation, reaffirmation or reception;

    b. appropriate lections to be used on the Sundays around the celebration or reaffirmation of baptism;

    c. prayers for the period before the rite;

    d. prayers for use by candidates' groups and in public worship for the period after the rite.

4. Prayers for parents and families during pregnancy.

5. Prayers and rites to surround the baptism of infants. These might include:

    a. a form for the welcome and support of parents and godparents preparing for a child's baptism;

    b. a pre-baptism prayer service;

    c. 'free standing' Sunday baptismal liturgy;

    d. rite of welcome and reception at the Sunday eucharist;

e. resources for use after baptism such as prayers for use in the home, prayers for use on the anniversary of a baptism, an order for an occasional service for those whose children have recently been baptised.

6. Appropriate material, for use with the rites of confirmation or reaffirmation, to acknowledge the transition into adulthood (paragraph 6.9).

The Place of the Bishop

The bishop's role requires the bishop, either himself or through others, to guide the Church in initiation :

  i. in focusing the mission and unity of the Church;

  ii. in teaching the faith;

  iii. in protecting and providing for the enquirer;

  iv. in affirming and praying for those coming to faith;

  v. in recognising the decision of faith (paragraph 7.4).

A bishop might offer a teaching module to parishes that could be used at an appropriate stage in the parish scheme of initiation (paragraph 8.5.6).

Where the more extended process of baptism is adopted as the agreed pattern within a parish, . . . it might be possible to follow the Roman Catholic practice of allowing presbyteral confirmation provided that the bishop was personally involved in at least *one* of the following ways:

presiding at the rite of call and decision in which a candidate was accepted for baptism, confirmation or reaffirmation;

involvement with the group during the extended period before baptism or related rite;

presiding at a rite of welcome into episcopal communion in the period after a baptism or related rite (paragraph 7.12).

PEOPLE ON THE WAY:
SOME STORIES

> **The welcome and nurture of new Christians is one of the most important tasks that faces the Christian community.**

Mary

Mary grew up in a Christian home. She was baptised in infancy, attended a Church school, was confirmed at 13, and has continued in the faith of her youth. She had a number of friends who were converted and subsequently baptised. Although she was confident in the reality of her baptism she missed some acknowledgement of her adulthood. She has been strongly influenced by a book of prayers which her auntie Jane gave her. Also at the time of her confirmation she had received a copy of the ASB ...

David

David was uncertain whether he had been christened. He knew next to nothing about the Christian faith until he went to university (ex-poly) to read architecture. The one active Christian group in the Students' Union was a Christian Union which used to run bar discussions and weekly Bible Studies. The curate from the local Anglican evangelical church sometimes came along. David enjoyed the Bible study and the sense of direction and belonging he experienced. When he split up with his girlfriend he prayed the prayer of commitment. The group told him that he should be baptised. He met the curate on campus and a conversation led eventually to his being baptised and confirmed as part of the Parish's Pentecost Praise. He wondered about his next move...

Penny

Penny really enjoyed going to church for the first time with the school last term. She thought the stained glass windows were 'magic'. There was a special smell about the building and she loved it when they had to sit in silence and look at the candle flickering on the altar. Now sometimes she goes into church after school just to be quiet. She thinks that it is almost as special as her secret den on the edge of Oak Woods...

Paul and Denise

Paul and Denise have been living together for four years. Paul, baptised as a Roman Catholic, had not been to Mass since he was eight and did not know whether he had been confirmed. Denise had been brought up in a church going home and attended regularly until she was fifteen. Neither of them thought much about the Christian faith until they got to know the couple next door who were regular attenders at the local Anglican church. They had interests in common and became good friends. They were impressed by the way this couple and their children looked after the old father who lived with them – and particularly by the difference that Christian faith made at the time of his death. Shortly after this they were invited to explore the Christian faith with a 'Good News Down Your Street' team. One thing led to another and here they find themselves before the bishop ...

Wesley

Wesley's parents liked his name but had never heard of the great Methodist preacher John Wesley. They did not know much more about the Christian faith. His father worked hard selling insurance; his mother taught French at the local school. His first job was with a local computer supplier and he was doing rather well. His main leisure interest was music and he developed a taste for jazz. At the jazz club he became friends with a man whose church ran a creativity workshop for mentally ill people in the neighbourhood and he went along occasionally. The centre was in an old church school and was backed by a management group from different churches who prayed for and supported it.

One day they were discussing the way in which black people in America found strength from the Christian story. He realised how little he knew. His friend mentioned that his church was keen to help people who wanted to look into the Christian faith. After a few evening gatherings at a nearby pub he decided that he would like to take a serious look at what the Christian life was about. His friend told him about the catechumenate programme Exploring the Way ...

Jean

Jean attended a Sunday School but stopped going when she was ten, feeling she had outgrown it. As a student she found her way into an Anglo-Catholic church and was moved by the beauty of the liturgy and by the down to earth friendliness of the congregation. Something deep in her was touched by the worship and she was impressed by the way people with learning difficulties seemed at home. She had little idea what Christians believed but started going regularly. She was asked to join a catechumenate group and introduced to Joyce a speech therapist who was going to be her sponsor. Father David explained that Mrs Wilson who only came to church when her arthritis allowed would be praying for her regularly ...

Colin

Colin has always wanted to be a bellringer like his father. Now that he's twelve he's just tall enough to begin to learn. There are three other youngsters in the team who are in their early teens. A new vicar has recently come to the parish and came to meet the bellringers one practice evening. There was an uncomfortable silence when he casually asked how many of them attended the services regularly and whether the young people had been confirmed yet.

A few weeks later the vicar announced that he was going to start a group for young people in the church (his own two children, three teenagers in the choir, the two eleven-year-olds who had just decided they were 'too old for Sunday School' and the young bellringers). The group would have a variety of activities, but over the next two years some of them might think seriously about confirmation. Colin would have liked to go with his friends but his father had made some rude comments about the vicar after his visit on the practice evening. He has not been baptized ... Does he belong or not?...

Don

Don is in his early forties. Once married, an increasing alcohol problem destroyed his family life and he was divorced twelve years ago. It took him another five years to admit his addiction and seek help, but since joining AA he has remained sober and begun to rebuild his life.

A few months ago Don heard one of the local clergy doing a 'Thought for the Day' on Radio 4. Both what he said and the way he said it attracted Don to seek out his church, although he had never been to church since childhood and had been extremely hostile to Christianity during the years of his addiction. Much to his surprise he enjoyed the service, found that the vicar more than lived up to his radio image, and became a regular attender. When a group started for other recent newcomers to the church to explore the basics of Christianity, Don was the first to sign up. He has begun to realise how he has already grown spiritually through the 12 steps of AA, and that God was with him even in the lowest depths of his alcohol abuse and marital breakdown. He can hardly wait to be confirmed!...

Zoe

Zoe was born last week. Her father goes to St Peter's, the Catholic church in the town. Her mother has always attended St John's and has such happy memories of Sunday School and the Youth Group. It hadn't always been easy having a foot in two churches. They had married in St John's with a special dispensation from the Roman Catholic bishop. Zoe's father had been asked to do all in his power to bring up his children as Catholics – but the priest had explained that this was not an absolute promise: the unity of their marriage was more important. Each of her parents would like Zoe baptised in their church and they each go to talk it over with their parish priests. They get the same answer from both: the place of baptism is not really important; what matters was where they intended to bring Zoe up. Things are made a bit easier by the fact that the churches are running a joint Parenting Course. It is friendly and practical; Zoe's parents find themselves having their first serious conversation about what faith is ...

John

John was baptised as a baby on the insistence of his grandmother. His parents had little interest in church. When a few of his friends started Sunday School they refused to let him go because it would interrupt their Sunday morning routine. John's passing interest soon waned and religion at school meant very little. He married in a registry office and his children were not baptised. At the age of forty he realised he was in a dead-end job and became dissatisfied with life. A friend from next door suggested he might find church helpful. In fact he found it totally bewildering but continued because his wife seemed to like it. Three years later he joined a nurture group and the faith 'clicked' for him.

Shortly after this he met some Baptist friends at work who showed him the Bible and told him that he needed to be properly baptised – by full immersion after making a public profession of faith. It all seemed very logical. In his innocence he approached the vicar who clearly found his request difficult to handle – his pastoral heart pulled one way and his theological knowledge the other: eventually he refused a second baptism. John went down the road to the Baptists where he is now a member (his wife still goes to the Anglican church)...

Stephen and Liz

Stephen and Liz were married five years ago in the parish church of the village where Liz's parents still live and where Liz was baptised. Her parents are not churchgoers, and since the village church had had no Sunday School or youth club,

9

Liz grew up without any contact with the church. Stephen's parents were active Methodists; he was a fairly regular attender of church and youth group when younger but became less regular in his last years at school.

They were thrilled and deeply moved when their first child – a daughter – was born six months ago; they felt a new sense of awe, gratitude and responsibility which they were very shy of talking about even with each other. Liz's parents began to ask when they were going to bring the baby 'home to be christened'. Neither Liz nor Stephen quite knew what they wanted. Stephen's parents told the couple that the decision about baptism was theirs alone but that they would support them in whatever decision they made: baptism was more than just 'a naming ceremony' and an excuse for a family party...

Liz talked about their dilemma to a friend she had met at pre-natal classes who went to the local parish church. The friend invited her to come to the Parents' and Toddlers' group in the church hall. There she introduced her to the curate who came to visit Stephen and Liz the next week. The curate reassured them that they were right to wonder whether baptism was right at the moment. She invited them to come, with the baby, to her home the following afternoon to meet a few local people who were, or had been, in a similar situation. They met together for a few weeks to look at where they were in their lives, to share experiences and questions and to find out a bit more about the Christian faith...

Bryan

Bryan joined Discoverers when he was ten. Although he had been baptised as a baby he could not remember ever going to church on a Sunday. The vicar used to take an assembly at school every Friday and sometimes all the children would go to church for a special service. He thought the vicar great fun and had enjoyed the Craft Day held in the church. Some of his friends belonged to Discoverers so one Sunday he arranged to go with them. He has been going ever since. At the next Family Service he is going to carry the Cross. His mother has said she may come as well...

Chapter 1

IDENTIFYING THE TASK

1.1 The welcome and nurture of new Christians is one of the most important tasks that faces the Christian community. It represents the meeting point of many different facets of Christian life. There is the personal journey and particularity of an individual coming to faith or exploring the reality of Christian life. There is the ongoing life of the Christian community represented by its gathering for worship and its dispersal in service and witness. There is the mysterious activity of God the Holy Trinity addressing and forming both the new believer in his or her journey and the welcoming Church in its encounter with new faith.

1.2 On 13th July 1991 the General Synod, in the context of a major debate on Christian Initiation, passed a motion at the request of the House of Bishops part of which asked

> the House of Bishops in consultation with the Board of Education, the Board of Mission, and the Liturgical Commission to prepare a paper on patterns of nurture in the faith, including the Catechumenate.[1]

This request recognised that many different areas of Christian discipleship are concerned in this very human activity of welcome and nurture. Evangelism, liturgy, education, and ethics (understood as reflection on the culture, patterning and distinctiveness of Christian life) all have a part to play. In modern Church life each of these tends to be seen as a distinct area with its own disciplines and skills, its own jargon and fads. Each of the areas of Church life has been the subject of considerable discussion in recent years at both official and unofficial levels in the Church. However if new Christians are to be welcomed, nurtured and incorporated, and if the Church is to be changed and enriched by those whom God is adding to its number, then these distinct worlds need to meet and interact. They face the demanding task of doing justice to the human and divine reality of God's new creation.

1.3 The 1991 Synod motion took up an earlier debate on 20th February 1990 initiated by David Hawtin, then of the Durham diocese, at which the following motion had been adopted,

That this Synod requests the House of Bishops, in the light of issues raised in the Knaresborough Report, to consider the case for reviving the catechumenate in order that adults, young people and infants may be associated with the Church, as a preliminary to Baptism, and for making provision for a draft order of service, whereby candidates would be admitted to such a catechumenate.

1.4   The proposer's own starting point had been a concern with baptism for families who had little contact with congregational life. However the motion and major speeches in the debate emphasised the broad pastoral potential of a catechumenate for adults.

1.5   As a result of the Synod motion of July 1991 a Group was drawn together under the chairmanship of John Dennis, Bishop of St Edmundsbury and Ipswich.

1.6   The Group has sought to understand and evaluate the catechumenate. This is a forbidding shorthand term for a phased and corporate approach to the Christian Initiation of Adults that has been pioneered by the Roman Catholic Church after the second Vatican Council and taken up in other parts of the Christian world.

1.7   In the light of its evaluation the Group sees the catechumenate as a positive model for Christian initiation. It welcomes the opportunity to attempt to provide an integrated overview of this vital part of the life of the Church. Although the last 300 years have seen enormous activity in presenting the Christian faith to individuals and preparing them for Christian discipleship, this has continued to be set within the formal framework fixed at the Reformation when Archbishop Cranmer linked the Catechism and Confirmation. This pastoral strategy, and its educational and liturgical consequences, are spelt out in the rubrics that follow the Catechism in the 1662 *Book of Common Prayer:*

> The Curate of every parish shall diligently upon Sundays and Holy-days, after the second Lesson at Evening Prayer, openly in the Church instruct and examine so many of the Children of the Parish sent unto him, as he shall think convenient, in some part of this Catechism.

> And all Fathers, Mothers, Masters and Dames, shall cause their Children, Servants, and Prentices, (which have not learned the Catechism,) to come to the Church at the time appointed, and obediently to hear and be ordered by the Curate, until such time as they have learned all that is here appointed for them to learn.

So soon as Children are come to a competent age, and can say, in their mother tongue, the Creed, the Lord's Prayer, and the Ten Commandments; and also can answer to the other questions of this short Catechism; they shall be brought to the Bishop: And every one shall have a Godfather, or a Godmother, as a witness of their Confirmation.

And whensoever the Bishop shall give knowledge for Children to be brought to him for their Confirmation, the Curate of every Parish shall either bring or send in writing, with his hand subscribed thereunto, the names of such persons within his Parish, as he shall think fit to be presented to the Bishop to be confirmed. And, if the Bishop approve of them, he shall confirm them in the manner following.

1.8   Archbishop Cranmer's Prayer Book of 1552 concluded this instruction with, 'And there shall none be admitted to the holy Communion, until such tyme as he can saye the Catechisme, and bee confirmed'. In 1662 this was softened to, 'And there shall none be admitted to the holy Communion, until such time as he be confirmed, or be ready and desirous to be confirmed'; a reflection, perhaps, that the bishops at least had found it hard to rise to the educational and liturgical demands of Cranmer's pastoral strategy.

1.9   The Prayer Book's strategy for the formation and incorporation of new believers might seem to many Anglicans today to represent a largely alien world. Its assumptions about educational process, about the way in which God wins people to faith, and about the social location and mission of the Church, are different from our own. At the same time it represents a seriousness about Christian nurture and about its proper integration into the public and sacramental life of the Church which we can recognise and respect. Even in Cranmer's time it was not without its critics. Martin Bucer criticised its dependence on the mere recitation of certain formulae,

And it is evident that not a few children make a confession of this kind with not more understanding of the faith than some parrot uttering his Hallo. So it would be far better to keep among the catechumens those children who as yet show no or only meagre signs of the fear of God and faith in their lives and manners ...[2]

1.10 As an official and integrated pastoral strategy the framework of the Prayer Book has yet to be replaced. Its separate concerns with Christian instruction, with bringing people to faith, with enabling people to find their place within the people of God, and with the mapping out of a personal and social ethic have all been taken up in very different ways.

13

The effect of this creative diversification however has been to create a distance between evangelism, education, ethics and baptism. This diversification or fragmentation has allowed many creative responses to flourish in the Church of England. It has contributed to a rich immersion in the life of the nation that might not have been possible if there had been tight central control on evangelism, education or ethics. But there is a price which has been paid in leaving these vital parts of Christian discipleship alienated from the sacraments with their important task of nourishing and ordering the corporate and individual life of Christian people.

1.11 The place this Reformation strategy gives to the rite of confirmation has provided a strong symbolic thread within Anglican life. Historically it seems that the first serious attempt to make episcopal confirmation fulfil the role envisaged in the Prayer Book came with the new pastoral bishops who received their personal formation within the evangelical and Anglo-Catholic movements in the nineteenth Century.[3] This was made possible by the greater ease of travel as well as the decreasing demands made on the bishops by the processes of Government. It also marked an attempt to make Cranmer's integrated strategy work at a time when his assumptions about the social location of the Church were probably losing even the appearance of plausibility. The ideals embodied in confirmation continue to have a potent resonance in the Church of England which has to be taken into account in the creation of any new integrated strategy for the formation and incorporation of new believers.

1.12 The centuries since the Reformation have seen a great amount of creative energy and initiative put into reaching the unchurched, proclaiming the gospel of Jesus Christ and nurturing new believers. Much of the initiative for this has rested with particular groupings or movements in the Church, and with the energy of particular parishes or voluntary societies, both Anglican and ecumenical. This means that there is considerable accumulated experience in this area to be found in the Church of England. Although the present state of faith in England is hardly cause for complacency it is clear that there are many effective points at which new believers are being helped and formed. However this wealth of activity still has to be fitted into a formal framework which reflects the pastoral strategy of the sixteenth and seventeenth centuries.

1.13 The Reformers' emphasis on instruction has continued to influence the way in which English Anglicans approached the initial formation of children and adults. Until comparatively recently confirmation preparation amongst both evangelicals and catholics followed a didactic approach forged initially for the intelligent teenager. However in the last twenty years new styles have emerged which follow adult-centred patterns that increasingly use agendas set by the enquirer. More emphasis is placed on the creation of a group life in which people can explore the experience of belonging and relate the content of the faith to their lives. Also more time is allowed for such groups – moving, for example, from the five to six weeks of earlier courses to the nine weeks of 'Saints Alive!' and the fifteen weeks of the Alpha course. Many of these developments echo the style adopted in catechumenal approaches to Christian formation.

1.14 Where the Reformation model takes the child as its typical candidate and instruction as its primary focus, the catechumenate approach takes the adult as its typical candidate and sets instruction within the wider context of experiencing the faith within the Christian community.

1.15 The initiative of the Roman Catholic Church in reviving a catechumenal approach to the Christian initiation of adults has allowed the Churches to explore this alternative framework or pastoral strategy for the nurture and incorporation of new believers. The Rite for the Christian Initiation of Adults (RCIA) was first published in 1972 and has been used extensively in various parts of the Roman Catholic world. A further impetus has followed the publication of a new English translation of the rite which is now in use in the Roman Catholic Church in England and Wales.[4] At least two Provinces within the Anglican Communion now also have extensive experience of this approach to adult initiation. In England the Catechumenate Network, with Peter Ball as one of its leading figures, has served to encourage experimentation in a number of parishes. The first formal Anglican appraisal of this approach appeared in the 1991 Toronto Statement from the Fourth International Anglican Liturgical Consultation.[5]

1.16 The Group watched together the Video *This is the Night* which portrays in a vivid way the use of the catechumenate in a Roman Catholic church in Pasadena, Texas, USA.[6] This brought home to the Group the way in which this approach involves both candidates and congregation in a progressive encounter which is robustly human and richly sacramental. Although the video portrayed a mixed-race 'blue-collar' parish from the mid-West of the USA, with a lavishness of celebration and a fervour in prayer which might shock many an Anglican congregation, it was easy to see that each of the main streams of English Anglican life would have felt at home in the processes it portrayed. The public character of its rites, perhaps initially disconcerting to the self-effacing character of the English, clearly plays a powerful part in giving the congregation a sense of its role in the welcome of new believers.

1.17 This new attempt in the Churches to take seriously an integrated approach to Christian nurture and incorporation not only provides an alternative overarching framework to the one we have inherited from the Reformation. It also takes as its typical candidate for baptism an adult rather than an infant. While the Churches are still assimilating the lessons of catechumenal approaches for adult initiation, only tentative steps have been taken into thinking through their implications for the incorporation and formation of those baptised in infancy. In chapter 5 of this Report we attempt to draw out some of the implication of this approach for the baptism and Christian nurture of infants.

1.18 The Liturgical Commission is currently reviewing the initiation provision of the Church of England. There are at least four stimuli for this review: the necessary review of the provisions in the ASB as its current period of authorization draws to a close; the motions passed by the General Synod in July 1991 on the subject of Christian Initiation; various matters previously referred to the Commission such as reaffirmation of baptism and rites of reconciliation; and the continuing ferment in the Church at official and informal levels about various matters concerned with initiation. The Group has recognised that its work is complementary to that being undertaken by the Liturgical Commission (and vice versa) and there has been close liaison between the two.

1.19 In chapters 2, 3, 4 and 5 of this Report we attempt to make available to the Church something of the thinking and experience which lie behind our proposals. In chapter 6 we set out our suggestions for the welcome, formation and incorporation of new Christians – adults and children. We see these not as a radical new framework but as a way of building on the diversity and acknowledged wisdom of current practice. We believe that the Church of England is now in the position to learn from the experience and wisdom to be found both within its life and elsewhere. Equally we believe that the Church of England will need to accept that, in the next stage of discovering and establishing a coherent approach to this important subject, provisionality and experiment are an inescapable part of the process. This will mean that, in any implementation of our proposals, there will need to be mechanisms for review and for fine tuning or development.

1.20 In chapter 7 we offer a framework and in chapter 8 we set out the pastoral implications of our approach.

Notes

1.   Full text of the motion carried is set out in Appendix 1.

2.   Censura. E.C.Whitaker, *Martin Bucer and the Book of Common Prayer* (Alcuin, 1974), p.104 cf J.D.C. Fisher, *Christian Initiation: the Reformation Period* (Alcuin, 1970), p.246

3.   Colin O. Buchanan, *Anglican Confirmation* (Grove, 1986), p.30. Peter J. Jagger, *Clouded Witness* (Pickwick Publications, 1982), pp.148-153.

4.   *The Rite of Christian Initiation of Adults*: Liturgical Edition for England and Wales (Geoffrey Chapman, 1987), Study Edition (St Thomas More Centre, 1988).

5.   David R. Holeton, *Christian Initiation in the Anglican Communion* (ed. Grove, 1991). See Appendix 2.

6.   Published 1992 by Liturgical Training Publications, Chicago. Available through McCrimmon Publishing Co Ltd, 10-12 High Street, Great Wakering, Essex, SS3 0EQ.

Chapter 2

ADULT INITIATION TODAY

> **Paul's conversion is not complete with the dramatic religious experience of Acts 9.3-9. It reaches its conclusion with verse 19, after the Church in Damascus has played its part in the welcome and incorporation of the new believer.**

2.1   There is more to becoming a Christian than joining a club. 'Unless one is born anew, he cannot see the kingdom of God.' (John 3.3) The mystery lies in more than the encounter with an unseen world; it includes the trauma of being caught up in the rebirth of the whole cosmic order. 'For anyone united to Christ, there is a new creation: the old order has gone, the new order has already begun' (2 Cor 5.17). The death and resurrection of Jesus Christ gave a new direction to human history; they marked the arrival of the end of an order dominated by sin and death. Jesus is God's final word not only of revelation but also of judgment and re-creation. When John the Baptist thundered over the baptismal water, 'Who warned you to flee from the wrath to come?' (Luke 3.7) his words point up the link between baptism and this world transforming trauma. The death and resurrection of Christ is not simply a vivid dramatisation of a recurring pattern in human life. Baptism is unrepeatable not because we cannot begin again; we often do. It is unrepeatable because Jesus is unrepeatable; the saving encounter with Jesus Christ draws us into the rebirth of a new world.

A Biblical Paradigm

2.2   The story of Paul's conversion in Acts 9.1-31 often functions as a model for adult conversion to Christ. It is sometimes seen as the classic text against which authentic conversion should be measured, although most of the main characters in the New Testament had less dramatic and more gradual journeys to faith than Paul. Paul's story often functions too as an unattainable ideal, demoralising Church and convert alike. Many Christians feel slightly guilty that they cannot point to some dramatic

18

moment when God turned them round. There is, of course, no reason to think that the story was intended to be treated in this way. A pastoral framework for supporting people coming to faith needs to recognise that most experience this as a gradual process. Nevertheless the passage does point to five important aspects of what is involved in Christian initiation.

Crisis. It is a background of crisis – disintegration and rebirth – which provides the context for Paul's encounter with the risen Christ. Verses 1 and 2 record the turmoil and anger which Jesus had brought upon the settled order or Jewish life. Paul is already caught up with responding to the arrival of the kingdom of God.

Conversion. Paul's conversion is not complete with the dramatic religious experience of vv. 3-9. It reaches its conclusion with v. 19, after the Church in Damascus has played its part in the welcome and incorporation of the new believer. The figure of Ananias and the unnamed disciples of v. 19 are integral to the story. The flow of the narrative includes five elements without which Paul's initiation would have been defective: welcome, spiritual discernment, prayer, baptism, and incorporation into the community of the Church.

Mission and Spirit. Paul's initiation does not mean docile socialisation into a static community (vv. 19-31). The passage gives a vivid account of a Church on the move – characterised by human warmth and loyalty, but also by conflict and upheaval as it found itself carried along by the shock waves of the resurrection. For Paul initiation meant being caught up in the mission of God's Spirit. For the Church it meant adjustment to the gifts and life of a new member. The scope of Paul's emerging ministry may have been unusual(!) but the pattern is normal: healthy Christian initiation includes expectancy and discernment about the gifts and call of the Holy Spirit.

Story. The passage indicates the importance of stories and story telling in Christian experience and therefore in Christian initiation. The story of Paul's conversion is told three times in Acts. Christian initiation cannot be reduced to doctrinal and moral instruction or liturgical rites, it must include the narrative of rounded human experience. Christian formation must allow an individual's story to be heard and to find its place within the unfolding story of faith in the Church and in the scriptures. There must therefore be appropriate space for the telling and retelling of human stories.

19

Journey and Pattern. It is while Paul is on the road that he meets the risen Christ. The idea of the journey is a major image of the narrative of scripture from the call of Abraham through to the itinerant ministry of Jesus and beyond. As an image of human life and of the passage to faith it allows both for the integration of faith with human experience and also for the necessity of change and development.

2.3   It is striking in this passage that the first Christians were known as The Way (Acts 9.2 cf. 18.25, 26; 19.9; 19.23; 22.4; 24.14; 24.22). As a name for life in the Christian Church, the term Way draws together three important dimensions of Christian discipleship: movement, integration and pattern. This last provides an important complement to the open-endedness of the idea of journey. Much New Testament Church life and instruction was about establishing appropriate patterns in the believing and living of Christian communities and individuals. In the New Testament the word *tupos* (pattern, example, imprint) points to this important dimension of Christian formation, cf. Rom. 6.17; Phil. 3.17; 1 Tim. 1.16; 1 Tim. 4.12; 2 Tim. 1.13; Tit. 2.7. The idea of communicating a shape to Christian gathering, believing and living occurs much more widely than the term itself. Satisfactory approaches to Christian initiation will need to reflect the dimensions of open-endedness, integration and patterning that are present in the idea of the Way.

Adult Initiation Today

2.4   Adult initiation is a common and growing experience in the Churches today. The Church of England alone baptised 8,900 people over 12 in 1992. In 1993 approximately 82 per cent of the 51,784 people confirmed in the Church of England were over 12; 45 per cent were over 16. The proportion of confirmation candidates over 20 more than doubled between 1973 (19 per cent) and 1993 (39 per cent).

2.5   The report *Finding Faith Today*[1] looked at the experience of more than 500 people from different denominations who 'made a public profession of faith' between March 1990 and March 1991. The study provides a picture of great diversity and vitality among those coming to faith as adults and looks in detail at many aspects of people's journey to faith. Among the conclusions drawn from this research are:

i. The great majority of people enter the Christian faith through a relationship. This could be a member of their family (29 per cent), one or more Christian friends (23 per cent), or a minister (17 per cent).

Only 4 per cent looked back to an evangelistic event as the most important help to them.

ii. It is impossible to stereotype people's spiritual journey by the sort of church they attended. It was found that in evangelical churches 63 per cent of adults coming to faith did not have the sudden experience of faith which was expected by the evangelistic methods used in those churches. Even more startling was the fact that 20 per cent of people in non-evangelical churches claimed they had a sudden experience of God. The average time for the 'gradualists' was four years with only one in five seeing their move to faith as taking less than a year.

iii. 'Nurture Group' training courses in preparation for baptism or confirmation were rated as helpful or very helpful by 95 per cent of candidates. The RCIA approach was even more highly regarded: the figure being 98 per cent.

iv. There is little 'sense of sin' among a majority of those coming forward as adults for baptism/confirmation.

v. The fellowship of the congregation and the friendship of the clergy were important factors in their spiritual journey. Most came to faith within the Church rather than finding faith outside it and then entering.

vi. Means of evangelism which do not rely heavily upon the communication of a verbal message are important. Many in the survey received the gospel at a non-cerebral level – through human relationships and pastoral care, through mystery and emotions.

vii. The numbers attending Sunday School/Junior Church, etc. are now very much smaller than in the period up to the end of the 1950s. Eighty-six per cent of young people have no contact with any Christian denomination at any point in their childhood.

2.6 A pastoral framework for supporting people coming to faith needs to recognise that most experience this as a gradual process. 'It is often assumed that younger people are more likely to have a sudden experience and advancing years means that a more gradual unfolding of God is more probable. Surprisingly the reverse is true. The "gradualists" on average began their process at the age of 30 while the average age for sudden conversions was nearly 36.'[2] Approaches to Christian formation should not treat the teenager as the norm. More care has to be taken to address the life experience and different starting points of those coming to faith.

21

2.7 A sizeable minority even of those from traditional Churches experience a sudden conversion. Where this is a response to a call to commitment it may well be a significant step on a lengthy pathway to faith. The paradigm from Acts 9 illustrates that, even where people have sudden experiences of God, it is important to provide frameworks and structures that allow those people to assimilate a pattern of Christian living, and to find their place within the Christian community.

Faith in Britain Today

2.8 Any pastoral strategy for helping people in their journey to faith needs to be based on a realistic assessment of people's starting point. Modern belief patterns are very different from those of the comparatively recent past. It is easy to assume that newcomers have a knowledge of the Christian faith and an experience of the Christian Church; this is no longer true for many people.

2.9 In his book *Church on the Move*[3] John Finney, the former Church of England Officer for the Decade of Evangelism and a member of the Group, proposes a diagram to give an approximate indication of the faith patterns in Britain today. This is reproduced in a modified form below:

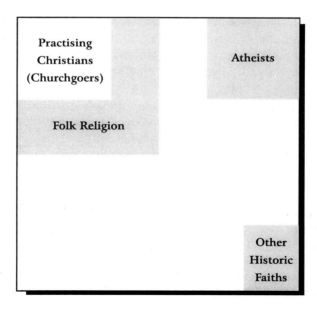

2.10 The smaller square in the top-left hand corner represents regular churchgoers who go to church two or three times a month at least. They form about ten per cent of the population. He comments,

> They are likely to be aware of the fundamentals of the faith and have some experience of prayer and the presence of God. However they are not to be taken for granted ... the Church must be a field of evangelism as well as the world. The Roman Catholic Church has understood this thoroughly and sees much of the first part of the Decade as being the evangelising of the Church. By this they do not just mean bringing people to a personal faith which corresponds to their baptism; they mean helping people so to get to grips with the gospel that they are living lights for Christ in the Church and the world.

2.11 The people represented by the larger area in the same corner are described as follows;

> Facetiously I call them the people 'who feel guilty when the minister calls', for their conscience tells them they ought to be in church. They are those who have a knowledge of the Bible, probably went to Sunday School or church in their youth, may still come to church for special occasions. They may well pray, and when they do it will be to God the Father through Christ. This group varies from one part of the country to another. Generally it is larger in the north than the south, in the country than the town, and in the suburb than the inner city or the estate. It is also markedly higher among the old than the young: in the 1950s more than 50 per cent of children had an active involvement with a Christian church – at the end of the 1980s it was down to 14 per cent. Young people in inner-city London are likely to have virtually no knowledge of the faith while elderly people in Cumbrian villages are likely to retain a good deal.

2.12 The book sets the number in the 'atheists' square at about ten per cent but many have suggested that this figure is too high. 'A thorough-going atheist who gives no ground to any superstition and who believes in nothing outside this world is not that common.' 'It is more common in the academic world than outside it, and possibly more common among men than women.'

2.13 Similarly the 'other historic faiths' corner is comparatively small. He comments,

> While the presence of other faiths is of great significance in some areas they are fairly limited geographically. There is some danger that we concentrate so much upon other faiths ... that we forget the much, much larger body of our fellow-countrymen and women who inhabit the remainder of the square.

2.14 These are some of his comments on those who occupy the central area of the box, marked 'The Rest':

> These people have virtually no knowledge of the Christian faith, yet many of them pray. When they swear they usually blaspheme 'Christianly' but know nothing of what or who they are invoking... Any bookshop shows the popularity of books on unusual happenings with the suggestion that they have some extra-terrestrial or supranormal explanation. Industrial chaplains report that a surprising number of top industrialists will not enter a major deal until they have consulted their clairvoyant ...

> This group comprises about half the population. The [person] who encounters those from within this group will need to remember that there are no resonances. A phrase like 'the cross' or 'the Good Samaritan' means nothing. It cannot be expected that the concept 'God' has any meaning whatsoever; 'sin' has no personal significance and 'life after death' is as likely to mean reincarnation as a more traditionally Christian view. Further those within this group are likely to have no experience of the Christian Church. If they came to church they would not know where to sit, nor the 'well-known' hymns, nor the difference between an old liturgy and the new. They may well not know the Lord's Prayer. A church is an alien and threatening land.

> This does not mean that they are particularly resistant to the message of Christ. Indeed because they are not inoculated they may respond better than those whose view of the faith has been tainted by some experience ... The evangelist cannot take anything for granted... This group may be forty or fifty per cent of the population, and it is growing. With them the Decade will succeed or fail.

2.15 The research behind *Finding Faith Today* showed that 33 per cent of adults making a public profession of faith come from the 'churchgoing' square, 45 per cent from the 'fringe', a handful from the 'atheists' and 'other historic faiths', and 20 per cent from 'the Rest' segment. It is obviously encouraging that people with little Christian background are being drawn to faith; it is not surprising that preparation of adult candidates takes much longer today than it did a generation ago. As many priests have commented, 'You have to start so much further back these days ...'

2.16 Provision for the welcome, support and formation of adults coming to faith in Christ needs to be shaped by a good understanding of the religious background prevalent in the culture. Many people will need bridge situations in which they can explore in depth and at their own pace many very basic aspects of Christian life, belief and practice.

Changing Perspectives on Evangelism

2.17 Not only does the Church of England have considerable and widening experience of adults coming to faith, there is also within it considerable evidence of a wider acceptance of evangelism or evangelisation as part of the Church's task, the development of more nuanced and adequate understandings of evangelism, and the development of courses and programmes and resources which find considerable acceptance across a breadth of Anglican traditions. A number of studies have noted the breaking down of barriers between different traditions in the practice of evangelism and Christian formation. Some of these developments will be noted in chapter 4. It is particularly significant that many of these approaches to initial evangelism and early Christian formation are now working with more holistic and gradual models of Christian growth. They are also recognising that the goal of evangelism has to include genuine incorporation into worshipping communities and a confident participation in Christian service in the world. There is a wider recognition of the importance of finding forms of evangelism that meet people where they are and of approaches to Christian formation or nurture that deal in an integrated way with Christian discipleship.

2.18 In the Church of England a major point of growth will continue to be contact with individuals and families arising from what has been called 'the creatively messy area where the pastoral and the evangelistic overlap'. The research behind Finding Faith Today showed that about 45 per cent of those finding faith saw pastoral contact with a minister as a significant factor. 12 per cent of men and 30 per cent of women saw their children, including the birth of a child or a request for their child's baptism, as a significant factor in their journey.[4]

2.19 This last group is important for any overview of approaches to initiation. *Finding Faith Today* comments,

> the evidence suggests that in practice parents need to be shown total welcome and also a way in which they can find out more about God in their own time. Many spoke of the three or four baptism preparation groups which they had been expected to attend as very formative... Further research needs to be done in this area to discover what is helpful to the parents and which method offers them an introduction and invitation to the Christian faith.

> The research shows that many found God through a sympathetic and helpful personal approach – not so much what happened at the service but in the

preparation beforehand and the follow-up afterwards... The number of [infant baptisms] in urban areas can be overwhelming ... It may be necessary to devise ways in which lay people can also make full use of these opportunities to serve members of the community.[5]

Requests for 'Re-baptism'

2.20 Requests for 're-baptism' are increasing, and obviously raise theological, pastoral and ecumenical problems. Clergy working with students have been known to keep a stock of Colin Buchanan's *One Baptism Once*[6] to hand as a standard pastoral resource. Such requests come not only from people whose family have no identifiable Church background or contact but also from those who want some public acknowledgement of an experience of God or a significant turning to God in later life. The motives for re-baptism vary: some reject their earlier baptism because they believe that they or others lacked faith; some see their earlier baptism as lacking in the public and dramatic character intrinsic to baptism. The impetus for these requests often arises from contact with baptist or pentecostal teaching.

2.21 There is some evidence of a change in the background of those requesting a second baptism. Such requests come not only from people in their twenties and thirties who have dropped away from church life after substantial contact in their childhood years. Many of those making this request have had no contact with any church during childhood and have not practised any faith until they are possibly 40 or 50 years old. When they find a faith for themselves the far distant baptism seems irrelevant. They have very little denominational loyalty and understandably follow the pathway set before them by those who have helped them come to faith.

2.22 This issue is not only a pastoral issue that arises in the initiation of those coming to faith. It is also a continuing source of tension in ecumenical contacts with Baptist churches, particularly in Local Ecumenical Projects. The mutual recognition of baptism has provided a breakthrough in ecumenical contacts, particularly with the Roman Catholic Church.[7] The 1982 Lima document *Baptism, Eucharist and Ministry* affirms:

'any practice which might be interpreted as re-baptism should be avoided'.[8] (paragraph 13).

However there are still difficulties as to whether this apparent consensus takes seriously disagreements about what constitutes valid baptism. Thus the Baptist Union of Great Britain and Ireland sees the Lima assertion as 'unacceptable', particularly 'in cases of infant baptism which are neither accompanied nor followed by any of the significant features of the initiating process to which the report amply draws attention.

2.23 A Report on a Consultation on Local Ecumenical Projects held in March 1994 by Churches Together in England made the following recommendations:

We recommend that Churches should strive for a more developed and disciplined catechumenate to ensure nurture in the Christian faith and to complete the whole process of initiation.

We recommend that there should be means and rites to enable serious and public affirmation of the Christian faith throughout life.

We recommend that those Churches which have a substantial involvement in LEPs should commission a high level group to explore a deeper understanding of baptism and to search with urgency for more comprehensive guidelines, and that extensive use should be made of the considerable experience – often painful, sometimes profound – within LEPs.

2.24 The consultation also proposed the following provisional guidelines:

Meanwhile, in the case of LEPs with a single shared congregational life and where there is Baptist participation, it would be inappropriate to re-baptise those who were baptised in infancy and who have already made a personal and public profession of faith in confirmation or formal admission to church membership. Those baptised in infancy who have not completed the process of Christian initiation and who, out of an instructed conscience, request baptism as believers should be placed under Baptist discipline and practice prior to baptism as believers and to reception into Baptist membership.

2.25 The once for all character of baptism reflects the once for all givenness of Jesus Christ (Eph. 4.4-6) and cannot be treated as negotiable in the initiation practice of the Church of England. The recurrent requests for 're-baptism' provide evidence of the failure of current patterns to give baptised people an awareness of their baptism. This points up the tenuous link that often exists between evangelism and baptism. It also indicates the absence of a strong baptismal theology in the liturgy and ongoing life of the Church of England.

Conclusion

2.26 Adult initation is a reality in Church life today and needs to be seen as deserving proper focus and attention. Increasingly there is a recognition that patterns are needed that take seriously the holistic approach to initiation implied in the biblical paradigm discussed at the beginning of this chapter.

2.27 In providing and planning for the Christian initiation of adults the following need to be taken into account:

i. The call of Christ to both individual and church involves disturbance and change.

ii. The goal of Christian initiation is incorporation into the people of God and active participation in the mission of God: membership of the body and service in the kingdom.

iii. Those coming to faith bring new gifts from God. The Church must be willing to change to receive them.

iv. Coming to faith involves a personal journey. It is the role of the Church to welcome the individual and to support them in this exploration.

v. People have very different starting points; these must be respected and allowed for.

vi. Space needs to be provided for the telling and retelling of people's personal stories and for discerning the presence and call of God in their lives.

vii. Christian initiation should integrate liturgy, living and believing, and enable people to assimilate usable patterns of worship, faith and life.

viii. The links between baptism and evangelism, and between baptism and Christian living, need to be recovered.

ix. Many people's lack of any knowledge of the scriptures or of Christian belief and practice has to be recognised. They need to be given time, resources and help in gaining a good basic grounding in these.

x. Churches need to address the question of how they can provide bridges for those outside the Church with little understanding of the Christian faith or experience of church life.

Notes

1. John Finney, *Finding Faith Today* (Bible Society/Churches Together in England, 1992).

2. *Finding Faith Today*, p.25

3. John Finney, *Church on the Move* (DLT, 1992).

4. p.40.

5. *Finding Faith Today*, pp.41-52.

6. Grove 1978, cf Michael Green, *Baptism* (Hodder, 1987), chapter 8. Gordon Kuhrt, *Believing in Baptism* (Mowbray, 1987), chapter 10.

7. cf *The Revised Ecumenical Directory of the Roman Catholic Church* (1993), pp.53-56 cf. *Unitatitis Redintegratio* (Vatican II Decrees on Ecumenism 1964) #3 and #22.

8. *Baptism, Eucharist and Ministry 1982-1990 : Report on the Process and Responses*, WCC No. 149, p.48.

Chapter 3

EVALUATING CATECHUMENATE APPROACHES

3.1   This chapter describes and evaluates an approach to the initiation and formation of new believers which is often called the catechumenate. A movement to adopt this approach to the initiation of new believers has been gaining ground in significant parts of the worldwide Church.

3.2   The word catechumenate itself continues to be a source of confusion. For many people, to catechize means to instruct and refers primarily to forms of oral instruction based on question and answer. The Greek verb from which it comes *katecheo* is used in a number of places in the New Testament (e.g 1 Cor. 14.19, Gal 6.6) and comes from the root *echein* to 'sound' or to 'ring'.

3.3   Thus a catechumen is one under instruction. In the early Church the term came to be used as a technical term for unbaptised people who were being instructed prior to baptism. At the time of the Reformation the term could also be used of baptised people under instruction.

3.4   The modern use of the terms catechumen and catechumenate has a somewhat different meaning, signifying not simply oral instruction but the whole process – social, spiritual and intellectual – that takes place in the corporate celebration of the sacraments of Christian initiation. The fourth International Anglican Liturgical Consultation at Toronto in 1991 described this process in paragraph 6 of Section 2 of its Statement (see Appendix 2) as follows:

> The catechumenal process begins with the welcome of individuals, the valuing of their story, the recognition of the work of God in their lives, the provision of sponsors to accompany their journey, and the engagement of the whole Christian community in both supporting them and learning from them. It seeks to promote personal formation of the new believer in four areas: formation in the Christian tradition as made available in the scriptures, development in personal prayer, incorporation in the worship of the Church, and ministry in society, particularly to the powerless, the sick, and all in need .....

3.5   The different meanings of catechumen and its cognates make the use of these terms difficult. In addition many feel that these terms will create barriers for the very people they are trying to help. We believe that the term 'enquirer' is less likely to alienate people but it is probable that the search for an acceptable vocabulary is not yet over. In this Report we attempt to follow the usage recommended in the Toronto statement, limiting 'catechumen' and 'catechumenate' to the unbaptised and using the term 'catechumenal process' for any process that follows the approach set out above.

The Roman Catholic Model

3.6 The Roman Catholic Church was effectively the first Church in modern times officially to adopt this approach to adult initiation and is the natural starting point for any assessment.

3.7 In 1972, as one of the reforms proposed in the Second Vatican Council, the Roman Catholic Church published *The Rite of Christian Initiation of Adults* (RCIA) with the intention of restoring 'an adult cate-chumenate divided into several stages'.[1] The impetus behind this reform seems to have come from two sources. One was missionary work in Africa, particularly by the Capuchin and Holy Ghost communities, which re-established a catechumenate in which preparation for baptism was marked out in stages, each step marking a progression in catechesis and conversion. The second was the ferment in Europe about the marginali-sation of the Church and the dawning recognition that this needed to be related to inadequate perceptions of the sacrament of baptism. One important influence was the restoration of the paschal vigil by Pope Pius XII in 1951 which had the effect of bringing sharply into focus the richer paschal understanding of baptism present in the practice of the ancient Church. Another was experimentation in France which led, for example, to the revival of adult initiation preceded by a short catechumenate in the Latin Quarter of Paris in 1957.[2]

3.8 A first English translation of the RCIA was produced by the International Commission on English in the Liturgy (ICEL) in 1974 and a new translation with a careful pastoral and theological introduction appeared in 1985. This was authorised for use by the Roman Catholic Bishops' Conference for England and Wales in 1987.[3] Since its publication this rite has provided the norm for adult initiation in the Roman Catholic Church. It has contributed to radical change in Roman Catholic Church life in North America and Continental Europe. It has led to the flourishing involvement of lay people as catechists and sponsors for those coming to faith and to the development of extensive aids for catechumenal groups. In many places it has had the effect of putting evangelisation and the initiation of new believers at the centre of the lives of many congregations as is well illustrated by the video *This is the Night.* Since the publication of an edition of the rites for England and Wales the RCIA is in use in virtually all dioceses, with about half the dioceses (12) having a diocesan rite of election on the first Sunday of Lent.

3.9   The RCIA has a number of significant features. One is its link with the Church's celebration of the death and resurrection of Christ (the Paschal Mystery) at Easter. Following the practice of the ancient Church in Rome the climax of this baptismal rite is the baptism of candidates during the Easter vigil as part of the Church's whole celebration of Easter.

3.10   The RCIA envisages the formation of the new believer as a journey taking place in four stages. During each stage they are supported by the Church and serve as a sign to the Church of the transformation implied in baptism. In particular the transition between the stages are marked by public rites. The Introduction to the RCIA describes the four stages as follows[4]:

– The *first* period consists of inquiry on the part of the candidate and of evangelisation and the pre-catechumenate on the part of the Church. It ends with the rite of acceptance into the order of the catechumens.

– The *second* period, which begins with the rite of acceptance into the order of catechumens and may last for several years, includes catechesis and the rites connected with catechesis. It comes to an end on the day of election.

– The *third* and much shorter period, which follows the rite of election, ordinarily coincides with the Lenten preparation for the Easter celebration and the sacraments of initiation. It is a time of purification and enlightenment and includes the celebration of the rites belonging to this period.

– The *final* period extends through the whole Easter season and is devoted to postbaptismal catechesis or mystagogy. It is a time for deepening the Christian experience, for spiritual growth, and for entering more fully into the life and unity of the community.

3.11   This outline, with its technical vocabulary, can sound forbidding and churchy. The reality as experienced is very different. The rites which mark the stages in the individual's growth are not elaborate and have the effect of supporting the person in their growth in faith. Each stage in the journey has its characteristic processes:

i. The period of initial enquiry is a 'no strings attached' experience in which Christians make themselves available, often to a group of people who have expressed some interest in the Christian way.

ii. The period of the catechumenate begins with the person being accepted as a hearer of the word of God and being signed with the cross before the Church. At this point a member of the Church accepts the role of sponsor and becomes their companion in the continuing journey. Pastoral formation takes place in two main contexts. They familiarise themselves with the life and worship of the Church by attending worship and being involved in its life. They also become part of a group which is guided by lay catechists, with the clergy acting at most as back up – and sometimes finding it difficult to adjust to their changed role. It is envisaged that from this point until baptism the groups withdraw from the liturgy after the liturgy of the word; they are hearers looking forward to more. Although not always practised, this dismissal is often welcomed as embodying a sense of anticipation felt by those involved.

The groups do not necessarily follow a set course; the content of these meetings is intended to arise from the shared stories and questions of the catechumens and reflection on the passages of scripture read Sunday by Sunday at the liturgy. This is not seen as a fixed period. People remain catechumens until they are ready after discussion to make a decision for baptism. During this period the catechumen is encouraged by the process to explore four aspects of the Christian way: the scriptures, worship, personal prayer and 'apostolic activity'. This last involves the beginnings of active service and witness.

iii. The 'rite of election' in RCIA, celebrated at the beginning of Lent, marks the decision to proceed to baptism. 'This step is called election because the acceptance made by the Church is founded on the election by God, in whose name the Church acts.'[5] In common practice this takes place before the bishop and is the candidate's prime encounter with his or her bishop. Within the process of formation this is often a time of some anxiety as the person faces the consequences of their impending public decision for Christ and the Church. The candidates for baptism then enter a period of intense preparation which is a sort of extended retreat. (In some places this includes an actual retreat, possibly attended by the bishop.) The focus for reflection in this period is the scriptures read during the Sunday liturgy in Lent. The Church supports the candidates with public prayer for repentance and deliverance, somewhat unhelpfully called by their ancient names of scrutinies and exorcisms. (We discuss the use of terms in paragraphs 3.32 to 3.34 below).

iv. The candidates are baptised with great rejoicing during the Easter vigil. They are also confirmed during this rite and provision is made for their being confirmed by a priest if the bishop is not present. During the Easter season up to Pentecost the group continues to meet. The function of these meetings is to reflect on the experience of entering the sacramental life of the Church and to prepare for entering more fully into the life of the Church.

3.12 Some may be attracted by the seriousness with which this scheme addresses the formation of new Christians and their integration into the life and mission of the Church. Others may be daunted by its structured character or nervous that it would distract those involved by its apparent ritual complexity. Within the Roman Catholic Church it seems clear that its primary result has been to create a flexible framework in which individuals, with their experience and needs, are taken seriously and in which they can explore the faith and grow in a way that is properly supported and that goes at their own pace. Part of its attraction is undoubtedly that it does not strait-jacket people into a pre-ordained course but creates a spacious framework in which they can find their feet as Christians.

3.13 The RCIA makes clear provision for sensible pastoral adaptation of its rites. (It also explicitly provides special simplified rites for the Christian initiation of children 'who have reached catechetical age').[6] In Roman Catholic circles considerable use has been made of this liberty. There were obvious gains in publishing a full and coherent set of rites. At the same time this has meant that there has not been much opportunity to incorporate the lessons of experience. There has been extensive adaptation both in liturgy and process in the years during which it has been in use in Catholic parishes – without the time or personnel to write up what is happening.

3.14 One particular difficulty, also mirrored in some Anglican experience, is that many enquirers are already baptised, raising the possibility of ignoring their baptism in order to fit them into the rites. The reality is that many people find the process represented by the RCIA a helpful way to reappropriate the Christian faith. This includes both baptised people who have never been fully initiated and also those who have become alienated from the Church.[7] A way needs to be found to allow groups of very mixed membership to function without treating the sacrament of baptism as an unimportant adjunct to the process. Where this happens it risks undermining the appreciation of baptism which should be one goal of the initiation process. The Roman Catholic Church in the USA has additional combined rites for welcoming the baptised but previously uncatechized adults into the full communion of the Catholic Church. Use of the American 'adapted rites' in some form is common in Britain.

The Anglican Communion

3.15 A number of Anglican Provinces are familiar with the office of catechist and have provision for enrolling people as catechumens. The Episcopal Church in the USA with the Second Edition of *The Book of Occasional Services* has taken the further step of publishing liturgical rites to frame a similar process to that adopted by the Roman Catholic Church. This book also provides a parallel framework for those who are baptised which begins with 'The Welcoming of Baptized Christians into a Community' and parallels pre-baptismal intense preparation with rites imitating the ancient practice of public penance. This Church now has considerable experience of this form of adult formation.[8] Anglicans in Canada are also exploring catechumenal approaches.[9]

3.16 The Toronto Consultation in 1991 provided the first opportunity for some sort of evaluation of catechumenal approaches to adult initiation from a wider Anglican perspective. The Consultation included not only a number of experienced practitioners but also Anglicans from the developing world with different experiences of initiation. This section of the Toronto Statement is reproduced in Appendix 2. In general the statement takes a very positive view of the potential of this approach. At the same time it gives careful consideration to particular criticisms or qualifications that have been voiced about the contemporary revival of the catechumenate.

English Anglican Experience

3.17 Within the Church of England there is now considerable experience of this approach particularly through the initiative of Peter Ball and the

Catechumenate Network. The first steps were taken in the 1950s with proposals by Ivan Clutterbuck for a 'Lay Apostolate', based on the experience of sponsors and catechists in France. In the 1970s Jim Cranswick introduced the method in the Kensington area of the London diocese. There are now about 75 churches in the Catechumenate Network and an increasing number of parishes experimenting with this approach.

3.18 Two books by Peter Ball have played a significant role in introducing people to this approach, *Adult Believing* (1988) and *Adult Way to Faith* (1992). He singles out five key emphases in this approach:

> *Welcome* as the underlying principle. 'The people who receive them and walk with them need to listen. Sometimes they need to learn to listen.'

> *Accompanied Journey* makes personal change rather than intellectual understanding the centre of the process.

> *Celebrations* within the ongoing worship of the Church in order to affirm the persons on their journey.

> *Faith sharing*, usually through story and dialogue, as an essential component in a person's appropriation of the Gospel story.

> *Community*, expressed through the involvement of congregation, sponsors, group leaders, catechists and clergy.

3.19 While not ignoring the liturgical dimension, this movement has concentrated on the potential for catechumenate groups of allowing an unforced growth into personal faith and discipleship. In practice the climax of the process has often been confirmation or re-affirmation of baptismal commitment, as many of those who join have already been baptised.

3.20 The experience of some 30 churches using a catechumenate approach has been monitored by David Sanderson of the Church Army. [A summary of this appears in Appendix 3.] This makes it clear that the approach has not only been of great help to individuals but has helped whole churches to own the process of evangelism and nurture.

3.21 It is interesting to note that churches in practice tend to diverge at one or more points from the theoretical model. For example the process does not always focus on Easter; not all the rites may be used; existing nurture courses may be used as part of the formation process. Often it becomes a year long programme starting in the autumn rather than an open-ended process moving at the pace of the enquirer. Such an annual programme still has the merit of involving the whole church but may indicate that it is not being used for those far outside the church.

3.22 Not only do churches give their own character to the way they implement this approach, but different proponents have different emphases. In the words of one Anglican commentator,

> Peter Toon looks for a clear biblical understanding of conversion, William Abraham stresses a here and now experience of the kingdom of God, Peter Ball puts the emphasis on relationships on the journey and Roman Catholics have a strong ecclesiology.

Evaluation – General

3.23 There have been many significant voices welcoming this approach as bringing important new elements to the formation and nurture of new Christians. In a powerful speech in the 1990 Synod debate Gavin Reid mentioned four gains: the dramatic reminder to congregations that 'they are in the conversion business', the use of lay people, the provision of a half-way house for people on the fringe, and the move away from a syllabus-dominated approach to Christian formation. Elsewhere he has called for evangelicals to move from a crisis model to a process model of conversion.

3.24 Another strong advocate of this approach is Robert Warren, the Church of England Officer for Evangelism, who has done a detailed study of the possible adoption of this approach within charismatic Anglican contexts. He sees defective initiation as the primary cause of the weakness of Western Christendom. He notes the similarity with what he calls the 'unconscious catechumenates' in charismatic renewal and also the 'catechetical implications of Alcoholics Anonymous & 12-step programmes in the USA'. He sees this approach as a necessary alternative to a 'bolt-on spirituality' in which people are never deeply rooted in the realities of the Gospel manifest in Church and kingdom. It is very much to be hoped that his rich and elegant study will be published in some form.

3.25 Similar points are made in the Toronto Statement's strong affirmation which emphasises similar points to those made above. In addition it comments that,

> It restores to the community of faith its essential role as the minister of baptism. It challenges the church through the questioning and enthusiasm of

new believers. It subverts the dominance of the clergy by recognizing the responsibility and ministry of all the baptised. (para. 7 of Section 2 – see Appendix 2)

3.26 On the more negative side, the Toronto Statement notes the importance of taking cultural context properly into account. It notes (para. 5 of Section 2), 'Patterns of formation vary greatly, taking different forms in isolated rural communities, societies where natural community is important and atomised urban society'. David Sanderson reports that some churches on council estates were unable to get the process started. Others have questioned whether the public character of the catechumenal process would make it viable in rural England.

3.27 It is clear that similar ideas on Christian nurture underlie a fine study *Growing New Christians: Developing evangelism and nurture in the local church*[10] by Steve Croft, Vicar of Ovenden and Wakefield Diocesan Mission Consultant. This thorough and practical book starts from a process or journey model of becoming a Christian. In noting the similarity between his approach and that of the catechumenate he raises three questions: Is it flexible? Is it simple? and Is there enough teaching? He objects, as many others have done, to the complex terminology which appeal to patristic practice has introduced. He questions the close tie-up of many forms of the catechumenate with the Christian year. He points to a danger that there may not be enough care given to the content of Christian teaching.

3.28 Common to the various catechumenal approaches is a recovery of the pastoral and baptismal dimensions of the bishop's role in the whole process of the initiation and formation of those coming to faith. (This is discussed in more detail in chapter 7.)

3.29 There are clear correlations between catechumenate approaches to Christian initiation and the biblical and pastoral insights explored in chapter 2. In general terms the Group endorses this approach to Christian initiation, judges that it corresponds to profound insights about human life and about the sacrament of baptism, and believes it can provide a useful model for better initiation practice in the Church of England.

Particularly welcome is the way it integrates evangelism, formation and liturgy. Some of the lessons of this approach are set out in *Five Elements of Christian Initiation. (opposite)*

FIVE ELEMENTS OF CHRISTIAN INITIATION

1. CHURCH. Initiation calls the church
to see itself as a baptised people
to welcome and learn from the enquirer
to be active in mission and service
to expect the anointing of the Holy Spirit
to walk with those seeking faith
to stand with the despised and oppressed
to look for the unity of God's people

2. WELCOME. Enquirers need a welcome
that is personal
that is public
that accepts their starting point
that expects the presence of God in their lives
that is willing to travel with them at their pace

3. PRAYER. Initiation involves prayer
for enquirer and church
to discern the presence of God
to open up to the grace of God
to support the process of change
to discover the moments of decision
to receive and recognise the gifts of God

4. THE WAY. Discipleship means learning
to worship with the church
to grow in prayer
to listen to the scriptures
to serve our neighbour

5. GOAL. The goal of initiation is
relationship with God the Holy Trinity
life and worship with the church
service and witness in the world

3.30 One benefit of moving to this approach to Christian initiation would be that it may begin to build bridges with certain Baptists and others who have been critical of Anglican practice and seen the absence of personal Christian formation as calling in question the validity of some Church of England baptisms.

3.31 At the same time there are various issues and qualifications which need to be noted and taken into account if the insights of this approach are to find a place in the life of the Church of England. It is to these we now turn.

Evaluation – Particular Issues

User-friendly terms

3.32 Many people find the terminology derived from ancient Christian practice archaic and forbidding, and see it as a barrier to the adoption of this approach to initiation. There is some evidence that the problem here may rest more with church people than genuine outsiders who are making the bigger step of entering an exceedingly alien world. The video *This is the Night* shows ordinary 'blue collar' Americans coping very cheerfully with terms such as 'neophyte'.

3.33 Great care needs to be taken in the area of language. In particular we suggest that the term catechumen should not be used in any official liturgical provision but that, following the example of Peter Ball and others, the term 'enquirer' could be adopted. Alternatives such as 'explorer', 'pathfinder', 'seeker' were considered, but each has other associations and seems too specific to carry the weight of extensive use.

3.34 One advantage of the term 'enquirer' is that it can be used with equal legitimacy of the baptised and the unbaptised. This would diminish the difficulty that has emerged with the Roman Catholic pattern and would make it easier for baptised and unbaptised 'enquirers' to explore discipleship together. However it is important that any rites do justice to the baptismal status of the individuals concerned.

The importance of baptism

3.35 One of the strengths of the Toronto Statement's discussion of catechumenal process is that it is set firmly in the context of baptism. The Churches are currently involved in a new exploration of the theological richness of baptism. Baptism is not simply a ritual starting line; it is a rich and fruitful sign of the Church's calling in Christ. In recent years there has been a rediscovery of the way in which baptism illuminates the Christian life and needs to be seen as a continuing point of reference within it. Thus the 1982 Lima Document sets out the richness of biblical imagery associated with baptism and explores five aspects of the meaning of baptism: Participation in Christ's Death and Resurrection; Conversion, Pardoning and Cleansing; the Gift of the Spirit; Incorporation into the Body of Christ; The Sign of the Kingdom. At the end of the initiation process the new believer should see baptism as a focus of assurance and identity.

3.36 This has implications for certain practices common in some forms of the catechumenate. There are strong reasons for not using terms or rites with baptised people which fail to acknowledge their baptism. It is also important that confirmation or some other rite should not be presented as a more important step beyond baptism.

This has important implications for any rites that may be adopted in the Church of England.

The Patristic Model

3.37 At the moment the Roman Catholic form of the catechumenate is serving as the model for other forms, particularly with its four stages and with its focus on the paschal mystery at Easter. Modern liturgical scholarship makes clear that this was not the only pattern of Christian initiation practised in the time of the Fathers.[11] Thus the great Church of Alexandria did not have such an elaborate form of catechumenate and at first did not allow baptisms at Easter. The Orthodox Churches of the East treat the Epiphany as an important baptismal season. This link with the baptism of Christ draws together important themes, in addition to the death and resurrection of Christ, which properly belong to a full baptismal theology: the revelation of the Trinity, participation in the kingdom of God, Jesus' identification with our sin in the water and in the baptism of his death, adoption as God's children, anointing with the Holy Spirit, etc.

3.38 The Roman Catholic catechumenate takes the form that it does because the Second Vatican Council decreed that Roman practice – that is, the custom of the city of Rome – should form the basis of liturgical reform in the churches of the Latin rite.[12]

3.39 Again this has implications for Anglican practice. It is not necessary to treat Easter as the only focus of the catechumenal process. While the involvement of the whole Church in the baptismal celebration is essential, there are good reasons, pastoral and theological, for also making other festivals a focus for such celebration. In the revised baptism rite being proposed by the Liturgical Commission there will be provision for major celebrations centring on Easter (Spring), on the Epiphany (January), on All Saintstide (November) as well as at other times ('ferial').

3.40 Furthermore the four-stage pattern generally adopted under the influence of Roman Catholic practice need not be seen as set in stone. There may be good reasons for developing other patterns. There is considerable evidence of other patterns emerging in the Church of England. This need not endanger the important principle which the catechumenate movement has rightly emphasised, that the journey into faith is one to which the whole Church must be visibly committed. For this reason we believe that the Church of England should make available flexible rites for those approaching baptism or the renewal of their baptismal commitment without either requiring their use or implying that a four-stage process is the only proper form of Christian initiation.

Are catechumens Christians?

3.41 There appear to be different possible understandings of what is involved in becoming a catechumen. The intention is to enable enquirers to approach their decision for Christ and baptism in a way that does justice to their developing faith and commitment. The decision for baptism is both a sign of faith and an act of faith: a sign that the grace of God is at work in a person's life; an act of trust which the Church must welcome, cherish and support. If the end of the process of initiation is clear, its beginning is less so. What is the faith status of a catechumen?

3.42 The Toronto Statement records (Section 2, para. 15) that

> Some believe that the catechumenal approach to baptism is in conflict with the New Testament practice of baptism on profession of faith. They think it may undermine the priority of grace made explicit by placing baptism firmly at the start of a person's public discipleship.

The question here is whether this stage in initiation is being used as a time of probation which improperly delays baptism.

3.43 This is an important issue with a number of strands that need to be unravelled;

i. The issue is complicated by the desire of Roman Catholic Canon Law to identify when a person is entitled to participate in certain rites of the Church, such as marriage. This leads to the difficult question, when does a journey begin? Without this preoccupation the focus would naturally rest on the goal of the process, baptismal incorporation. Thus the Introduction to the RCIA says , 'Joined to the Church, the catechumens are now part of the household of Christ'[13] although they are not yet baptised and do not receive communion. Again it says that 'the prerequisite for making this first step is that the beginnings of the spiritual life and the fundamentals of Christian teaching have taken root in the candidates'.[14] At the rite of acceptance the catechumen is asked some such question as 'What do you desire?' and possible answers include 'The grace of Christ' or 'Entrance into the Church'.

ii. Pastoral practice indicates that the significant time of decision and turning is not the moment when a person becomes a catechumen, but rather 'election', the moment when a person becomes a candidate for baptism. Clergy report that this, rather than the night before the actual baptism, is when candidates (or parents) ring up in panic. This would suggest that the stage of being a catechumen needs to be seen as the last stage of being an enquirer rather than a first instalment of baptism. We therefore believe that any Church of England provision be structured and presented so as to treat 'election' (as in RCIA) as the significant moment of decision. This would take up the stage in the process represented in the present ASB Baptism Service by the section headed The Decision.

iii. Where people have little Christian background or none, an extended period as a catechumen is likely to be appropriate and an over-hasty baptism may deprive the person of some of the riches that they can appropriate from a slower celebration.

iv. Any suggestion of a period of probation must be avoided, particularly as there is some evidence that the catechumenate has been used in this way in the past, not least in overseas mission. There are two dangers that can arise from treating the catechumenate as a period of Christian probation.

The first is that it may undermine the principle of grace by implying that certain moral or cultural standards have to be reached before a person can receive Christ. Christian behaviour is not a precondition for receiving Christ; it is made possible by receiving Christ. Reliance on grace is the mainspring of Christian living and must not be undermined in the process of initiation.

The second danger is that the Church may try to use the practice of probation to preserve its cultural commitments or social standing. One of the main critiques of missionary practice, found in the writings of Roland Allen,[15] was the difficulty the missions had in taking the risk of trusting the grace and Spirit of God. He highlighted the subtle tendency to make educational or cultural conformity a precondition of discipleship.

A person's time as a catechumen or enquirer draws to an end with a period of mutual discernment in which individual and Church seek the mind of the Spirit as to the way forward. Both church and candidate will lose out if this becomes a pressure to mere social or cultural conformity.

v. The underlying assumption of this approach is that baptism – like the initiation it expresses – is not a mere isolated moment but a rich sacramental process, focused in a particular action, that requires time and attention for its proper appropriation. This is important for the candidate. It is also important for the Church as 'the Church as well as the candidate must be fully and meaningfully present for the sacramental act'.[16] This means that the period from 'election' should be seen not as a stage in the 'preparation for an eventual baptism, but as part of the extended process of baptism'.[17] Again this should be made clear in the way any Church of England rites are presented.

vi. The biblical paradigm of Acts 9 explored in chapter 2 supports the belief that baptism and incorporation into the community of believers are part of conversion and not a supplement to it.

Syllabus, scripture, patterning

3.44 The question has already been raised whether the subject matter for catechumenal groups should arise purely from the personal lives of those involved in dialogue with the scriptures being read in the assembly. David Sanderson's investigations have shown that many churches involved with the catechumenate do in fact use one of the various courses currently available. *Finding Faith Today* found that while the very open-ended approach of the RCIA was appreciated by some there were many who would have preferred a more systematic approach; thus one participant said,

> It could definitely be improved by teaching more about the Catholic religion – this was strongly felt by all converts and was even expressed at the diocesan meeting from all groups taking part. (57-year-old housewife)

3.45 These concerns need to be taken into account. Furthermore some wish to ensure that the emphasis on intellectual enquiry, which has been part of the Anglican heritage, should still find a place. Clearly it would take considerable skill to draw out the breadth of Christian insight on belief and behaviour, not to mention the complex story of the Church, from the Sunday readings. It is not surprising that catechumenal group leaders turn with relief to the excellent course material available. It is likely that some parishes may need to give a higher priority to making resources and training available to those who lead such groups.

3.46 At the same time there are important insights in the theoretical model of the catechumenate which should not be lost.[18] If the adverse comment indicates that people find it hard to begin an open dialogue with the scriptures, this may be evidence that the 'pure theory' should be given more chance to work. It is a vital part of Christian formation that people develop confidence to dialogue with and feed from the scriptures.

3.47 For the Sundays before a baptism the lectionary in use in the Roman Catholic Church is explicitly chosen to throw light on the themes of cleansing and illumination. The Liturgical Commission intends to provide appropriate sets of reading for the Sundays around a baptism so that at least during this period church and candidates can together reflect on the scriptures.

3.48 Another source of content in the patristic tradition which underlies the RCIA is the formal handing over of the Lord's Prayer and the Creed. This takes place on the Sunday before the baptism, which may be too late to contribute to the content of formation. However there is wisdom in the practice of using such central texts as a way of patterning belief or prayer. This may need to be explored further. We recommend that the Lord's Prayer, the Apostles' Creed, Jesus' summary of the law, and the Beatitudes be available as texts which could be taken as a liturgical focus for formation.

How important are the rites?

3.49 A number of churches have initially been reluctant to adopt many – or even any – of the rites associated with the catechumenate. Their main concern has been to avoid embarrassment for those who are coming to faith. However the decision is often regretted and reversed in later years. Experience shows that liturgical rites are an integral part of the process. The marking of a person's growth in faith, and the involvement of the congregation with them in prayer, play a vital part in supporting an individual during a time of change and enabling the congregation to be committed to the journey the person is making. The rites both open up those involved to the grace of God and confirm the public character of Christian discipleship.

Sponsors

3.50 An essential part of the Faith Journey as envisaged in the catechumenate is that it should be an accompanied one. The role of 'sponsor' is therefore highly significant. Essentially it is an Emmaus Road experience. The candidate and sponsor walk together. The sponsor – a lay person – cares for and prays for the candidate and introduces the candidate to the rites. The sponsor shares his own faith journey and helps the candidate to articulate and thus evaluate and value his own. In most circumstances sponsor and candidate are both members of a group. But the pattern also allows for, and gives space to, those who temperamentally are not group minded.

Family catechumenate?

3.51 Catechumenal approaches have arisen as the Church faces its responsibilities to adults outside the life of the Church and on a journey to faith. The RCIA takes as its typical candidate an independent adult. Comparatively little work has been done on relating this model and its fundamental insights to the initiation and formation of children growing up within the life of the Church. A further important question is whether it offers a legitimate model for the welcome and nurture of families with little Church connection who bring infants and young children for baptism. These questions are addressed in chapter 5.

Flexible development

3.52 Part of the underlying philosophy of the catechumenal approach to Christian initiation is that the process involves the Church in growth and change. This principle will apply in turn to official provision of a framework of rites. The Church will be beginning a journey the end of which is not yet known. First attempts to create space for this approach will inevitably be flawed and will need to be adapted in the light of further experience.

Questions of culture

3.53 One of the Toronto Consultation Recommendations reads,

> The catechumenate is a model for preparation and formation for baptism. We recognize that its constituent liturgical rites may vary in different cultural contexts.

3.54 A number of important questions cluster around the relationship of the catechumenal process to culture –

i. Cultural factors need to be taken seriously in deciding whether or how to adopt a catechumenal approach to Christian initiation. Steve Croft has a useful chapter identifying important questions about local culture that need to be addressed in setting up a group approach to Christian nurture.[19] His story of two possible outcomes in an attempt to establish a group (see Appendix 6) shows what may be at stake in addressing the question of culture.

ii. There is a concern that

> it will raise barriers between the Church and the surrounding culture. Some are anxious not to alienate those who are associated with the church as God-fearers... Properly practised, the catechumenal approach to baptism can lower barriers between Church and society in two ways: first, it creates a bridge to enable people outside the Church to find their way in; second, it encourages the Church to value and respect the cultural heritage of those coming to faith.' (Toronto Statement, Section 2 para. 16).

iii. The Christian faith has shown a considerable ability to create and shape culture. The public nature of some of the rites associated with this approach may play a part in shaping expectations within local cultures.

iv. There is an inevitable element of inculturation in implementing a catechumenal approach to initiation. This may bring to the fore the diversity of local culture. This is an important issue which needs to be faced by many Churches in Britain today. The Toronto Statement says of this approach that, 'it respects the integrity and humanity of those seeking faith and avoids the danger of squeezing them into a pre-arranged and scheduled programme' (2.7). Again, 'It will also provide an important foundation for allowing different Christians their true and just place within the life of the church. This is of particular significance for categories of Christians who are marginalized by church or society.' (2.9)

Conclusion

3.55 The Group believes that a catechumenal approach to Christian initiation reflects important theological and pastoral insights about initiation, and that many elements of this approach are already present in much of the best practice in the Church of England. The catechumenal approach provides a useful model against which to review and improve initiation practice in the Church of England. In such a process the following points will need to be borne in mind:

a. The use of terms needs to be carefully considered (paras. 3.5, and 3.32 to 3.34).

b. The rites and process of initiation should take seriously the baptismal status of individuals and help both individual and Church to see baptism as a focus of assurance and identity (paras. 3.35 and 3.36).

c. Flexible rites should be made available for those approaching baptism or the renewal of their baptismal commitment without either requiring their use or implying that a four-stage process is the only proper form of Christian initiation (paras. 3.37 to 3.40).

d. Any provision should be so structured and presented as to treat 'election' as the significant moment of decision (para. 3.43 ii).

Notes

1. *Constitution on the Sacred Liturgy* 64
2. Aidan Kavanagh, *The Shape of the Liturgy* (Pueblo, New York, 1978) pp.93-97 cf. *Pour une memoire catechumenale* Pascal Thomas, Croissance de l'Eglise 1992.
3. Liturgical edition (Geoffrey Chapman, 1987); study edition (St Thomas More Centre, 1988).
4. RCIA Introduction 7

5. RCIA 106

6. RCIA, pp.149-185 cf *Issues in the Christian Initiation of Children : Catechesis and Liturgy*, ed Kathy Brown & Frank C. Sokol (Liturgy Training Publications, Chicago 1989).

7. cf. S Harmony *Re-Membering : The Ministry of Welcoming Alienated and Inactive Catholics* (Minnesota, Liturgical Press 1991).

8. cf *The Catechumenal Process*, Office of Evangelism Ministries, The Episcopal Church (The Church Hymnal Corporation, New York, 1990). *The Baptismal Mystery and the Catechumenate* ed Michael W Merriman (CHC, 1990).

9. John W.B. Hill *Making Disciples : Serving Those Who are Entering the Christian Life* (The Hoskin Group, Toronto, 1991)

10. CPAS 1993

11. Paul Bradshaw, *The Search for the Origins of Christian Worship* (SPCK, 1992) pp.161-184 cf. Essays in Early Eastern Initiation (Alcuin/GROW 1988), pp.5-17.

12. *Constitution of the Sacred Liturgy* 38

13. RCIA 47

14. RCIA 42

15. *Missionary Methods : St Paul's or Ours?* (1912). Reprinted with foreword by Lesslie Newbigin (Eerdmans, 1983); *The Ministry of the Spirit,* ed D.M.Paton (London, 1960); *The Compulsion of the Spirit : A Roland Allan Reader,* ed David Paton & Charles H. Long (Eerdmans, 1983).

16. Toronto 2.15.2

17. Toronto 2.15.2

18. cf J.B. Dunning, *Echoing God's Word,* Washington Forum Publications (Liturgical Training Press, Chicago, 1993/4).

19. *Ibid* chapter 6.

Chapter 4

THE FOUR STRANDS

4.1   Behind the implied pastoral strategy of the Book of Common Prayer and the catechumenate movement's approach to the Christian initiation of adults lie a common desire to bring four separate strands of Christian life into relationship with each other. These are Evangelism, Education, Liturgy, and Ethics. In considering the way forward for the Church of England it is not possible to propose an integrated approach from scratch. It is necessary to take seriously the current state of play in these four separate areas. Within each strand it is possible to identify themes or conflicts which have an impact on any overall pastoral strategy for the formation of new Christians.

1 – Evangelism

> *Those who see faith coming through developing spiritual awareness face a culture in which many are open to various forms of diffuse spirituality but who are reluctant to make the full Christian commitment of lifelong service of God and neighbour, and are nervous of entering the community of the Church.*

Pastoral care or evangelism?

4.2   'The supreme judgement and last resort is to the Prince and not to his Clerks'[1] (Bishop Jeremy Taylor 1613-1667). The Reformation bequeathed the country an ideal in which the Civil Power has a responsibility to provide for, and to protect, the spiritual (i.e. religious) welfare of its subjects, and in which the Church has a responsibility for the pastoral care of the nation and all its citizens. On this view the institution of the Church is perceived as a sort of religious National Health Service. Although a culture which sees religion as a private matter finds such a notion difficult to understand or accept, it continues to be present and to shape perceptions both in the nation and within the Church. The Church of England still sees its vocation as serving the body of English people. The resonance of this ideal still gives the Church of England wide access in English life. It creates many of the Church of England's best opportunities to commend personal faith in Jesus Christ.

4.3   Jeremy Taylor described the Church's role as spiritual rather than political and gave this description of her task:

> Thus the Church hath power to command us to be devout in our prayers, to be charitable to our Brother, to forgive our enemy, to be heartily reconciled to him, to instruct the ignorant, to follow holiness, and to do justice, and to be at peace with all Men.

4.4   This represents a vision of pastoral care that is much deeper than mere 'tea and sympathy'. However it sits uneasily with three important aspects of evangelism: conversion, vulnerability, and the challenge of the kingdom of God.

4.5   Two strands lie behind historic Anglicanism's difficulties with the idea of conversion. The first is theological. In common with Augustine and moderate Calvinism it lays strong emphasis on grace as the moving force behind individual repentance and faith (cf Article X): on this view, what people often call 'conversion' is not the beginning of a Christian life but one stage in the work of the Holy Spirit in that person's life. Secondly the Anglican Reformation ideal did not envisage citizens outside the Church. The right of English citizens to dissent from the country's understanding of the Christian faith was established with great difficulty over the following centuries. They found it even harder to put themselves beyond the reach of the Church's high vision of pastoral care. These two factors, a national vision and an emphasis on the hiddenness of God's work, have led to a certain resistance to the idea of conversion. It may make it hard for the English Anglican psyche to identify certain individuals as enquirers or catechumens.

4.6   The English Anglican pastoral ideal has often led to heroic commitment by many clergy to the poor and vulnerable in society. At the same time it has made it difficult for the Church of England as institution to come to people as the vulnerable ambassador of a Gospel of reconciliation. 'I was with you in weakness and in much fear and trembling' (1 Cor. 2.3) is probably how many bishops and clergy feel, but this can conflict with the public perception of their role as guardians of the nation's moral and spiritual health. Many clergy are skilled at combining the roles of vulnerable ambassador and community pastor. The public image of the Church of England has not found this double act so easy to manage. Identifying certain people as enquirers will both threaten and clarify roles.

4.7 The ideal embodied in the Reformation settlement has also complicated the Church's ability to challenge the individual to respond to the Lordship of Christ. Jeremy Taylor insists, 'It is not lawful for the ecclesiastical power to excommunicate Christian princes, or the supreme civil power.' It was said of the first Christians that they preached 'another king, one Jesus' (Acts 17.7). These two positions can be reconciled, as the long tradition of Augustinian political thought has shown. At the same time the tension between them can disable evangelism. Biblical evangelism is not just the offer of forgiveness and heaven, it is the proclamation of the kingdom of God; it involves a summons to a clear public allegiance. A public catechumenate would make this challenge visible.

4.8 The Church of England's continued allegiance to the ideal of pastoral care has been complemented at an unofficial level by a wealth of different evangelistic strategies and organisations, representing a variety of different traditions. The absence of an official framework within which the conversion and formation of adult converts can be located has encouraged a wealth of creative and culturally sensitive approaches. However it has had the dis-advantage that these have tended to remain somewhat detached from the public life of the Church. It has therefore been harder for the Church itself to acknowledge such activity or to welcome and learn from those affected by it. The time has come for recognising and supporting enquirers; official provision will need to be flexible enough to relate to current forms of evangelism.

The debate about evangelism

4.9 The Lambeth 1988 summons to a Decade of Evangelism has brought into the open many anxieties and debates about evangelism. It may be helpful to chart some of the issues that emerge. At the same time there is evidence that open discussion and practical experience are reducing anxiety and leading to the mixing of positions and more rounded views of the Church's responsibility to those outside, or on the edge of, its life.

4.10 One debate has concerned a possible difference between evangelism and evangelization. Some see the words as synonymous. However, for many Catholics 'evangelism' is irretrievably linked with hard-sell evangelical missions, often with a right-wing political stance. 'Evangelization', on this view, describes personal and corporate renewal through the action of God in the life of the world. Many non-catholics are reluctant to allow 'evangelism' to be defined so narrowly and see it as the work of God through his Church in both individuals and society. Others see evangelism as focusing on the individual and evangelization on society.

4.11 Debate has also concerned the nature of individual conversion and this is reflected in different emphases and strategies. At some risk of caricature three common approaches can loosely be related to three New Testament words:

'Good News': Evangellion. This approach concentrates on the preached word and sees the 'decision for Christ' as the essential element. There is a high cerebral content: the message has to be understood and believed before a response can be made. Evangelism is helping people to hear so that they can understand. Six to ten-week courses introduce the convert to the essentials of the Christian life as well as allowing them to reflect on the experience they have had and see how it challenges their previous lifestyle. The Church is often seen as a secondary or negative part of the package. Considerable energy and resources can be spent on organising evangelistic events.

'What is Taught': Didache. The emphasis here is on content, with evangelism seen as educating people to know what the Christian faith is. In this approach intellectual apprehension and incorporation into the Church and its worship require an extended process of instruction. For young people it is hoped that school will educate people into faith. For older people extended courses lead to baptism or confirmation. The institutional expression of this approach tends to be expenditure on church schools and parish instruction and education programmes.

'Reality Revealed': Mysterion. This approach sees coming to faith primarily as the revelation of God to the human personality through the work of the Spirit. Faith comes less by words and more through friendship with a Christian, encounter with God through music or painting, the presence of God in worship and especially through the sacraments. Elements of this approach are found in different ecclesiastical traditions. It often places less emphasis on formal processes of initiation. At parish level priority is given to making available a range of different kinds of experience or devotion.

4.12 During the early years of the Decade each of these strands has become less distinct. In part this arises from a consciousness of a common failure to make much impact in modern England and a greater willingness to begin by listening rather than talking. The different traditions are beginning to learn from each other.

4.13 Each of the three approaches has faced difficulties which point to the need for new and more holistic approaches to Christian initiation.

4.14 The 'decision for Christ' approach is facing up to the difficulty of communicating in a society where knowledge and experience of the Christian faith is increasingly rare but where there is considerable interest in the 'spiritual'. Results tend to be limited to those already in contact with the Church.

4.15 Similar uncertainty exists about reliance on education.[2] Some advocate more evangelism in school; others question whether schools are the right environment for Christian faith to be assimilated. For the Christian faith to be acquired and practised something more like apprenticeship is needed; people need a mixture of imitating a particular Christian, or group of Christians, and reflecting upon that experience in the light of the scriptures, Christian instruction and human experience.

4.16 Those who see faith coming through developing spiritual awareness face a culture in which many are open to various forms of diffuse spirituality but who are reluctant to make the full Christian commitment of lifelong service of God and neighbour, and are nervous of entering the community of the Church.

4.17 Debate and experience are refocusing the Church of England's commitment to evangelism In addition to more integrated forms of parish based evangelism, some are experimenting with congregations which take as their total starting point one or more of the cultures that now exist outside the Church; one example is the 9 o'clock service in Sheffield. Another significant movement is attempting to stage 'seeker services', influenced by the strategy of Willowcreek church in Chicago which tailors its public presentations as a kind of corporate catechetical ladder to enable individuals to come to faith at their own pace. Some of these developments could be seen not simply as commendable attempts to engage with contemporary cultures but as expressions of despair about the capacity of present congregations to provide a home for those outside the Church. Catechumenate approaches represent a different strategy for helping outsiders cope with Church culture and helping congreg-ations adjust to cultural changes. Its emphasis on the welcome and support of the individual enquirer can create the dynamic for deeper engagement with non-Church cultures.

4.18 Particularly significant are various attempts to see evangelism as requiring initiation into a new mode of living that is itself deeply rooted in communities which are deriving their vitality from the Gospel. This involves addressing the re-integration of evangelism and baptism. Thus Robert Warren,

> An essential ingredient of true initiation is initiation into the believing community... It is therefore necessary to find ways of re-initiating the whole Church, and re-tooling it to be sustained in living out a baptismal spirituality... baptism marks a point of departure, not arrival.

2 – Education

> *Congregations and dioceses must take much greater responsibility for the formation of Christians.*

A Christian family:

(a)   seeks to live by the teaching and example of Jesus Christ;

(b)   joins in the worship of Almighty God on Sundays in church;

(c)   joins in common prayer and Bible reading, and grace at meals;

(d)   is forgiving one to another, and accepts responsibility for one another;

(e)   shares together in common tasks and recreation;

(f)   uses abilities, time and possessions responsibly in society;

(g)   is a good neighbour, hospitable to friend and stranger.

Lambeth Conference 1958

4.19 The term 'education' has a broader reference than the activity that goes on in schools, colleges and universities. Even in the narrower sense there is at the moment considerable ferment and change. Alongside the moves to return to a more 'traditional' agenda in the education of young people, there is a creative diversification of the places and types of educational opportunity available to people. There is also a welcome development of partnership between educational institutions and the wider community which may lead to more radical changes of perception about education and people's potential. People's experience of education is a formative influence that needs to be taken into account in Christian initiation. Approaches to education in society clearly interact with the educational task of the Church. Faced with a subject of such breadth we identify three areas that are relevant to Christian initiation and formation.

What part should schools play in Christian formation?

4.20 To some people this question may be a surprising one. Many Christians have little understanding of, or perhaps sympathy for, Church involvement in schools, although this may be changing as the 1986 (No 2) Education Act involves more ordinary citizens in the expanding responsibilities of School Governors.

4.21 In Old Testament cultures, education – the communication to young people of ethos and know-how, skills and information – took place within the ordinary institutions of society, the home, the city, the civil service, etc. By New Testament times the situation was different. Not only did Greek culture place great emphasis on gathering young men together for education, but the synagogue had adopted a similar approach in imitation of the Greek pattern.[3] Synagogues were primarily places of study, as the Yiddish term *shul* indicates; study was not restricted to adolescence and in Jewish culture was dominated by oral dialogue with written texts.

4.22 The early Church gave a high priority to the instruction and formation of Christian believers, as the existence of the New Testament itself indicates. The primary context was the life of the Christian community into which converts were incorporated. Instruction meetings were held and the position of catechists emerged. Christians' commitment to teaching played a significant part in a move within the culture from the scroll to the more convenient codex or book.[4]

4.23 After the conversion of Western Europe the Christian Church adopted a strategy which enormously shaped Western culture. Schools were created and controlled by the Church. Until at least the seventeenth century they were seen as a branch of the Church. The syllabus, shaped by the desire that people should know and be formed by Christian belief, focused on the scriptures and Church teaching. (The word trivial comes from *trivium*, the three ways – referring to the basic medieval syllabus of grammar, rhetoric and logic which were seen as the necessary equipment for theological study of scripture.)[5] From early times this led to two emphases that have tended to pull against each other: the desire to teach the Christian faith, and a sense of responsibility for giving people a broader human education. Even in the nineteenth century something like the same dynamic – with the same tensions – was at work. Up until the 1870 Education Act the major source of funds for schools in England came from church people.[6] Sunday Schools were created as a way of providing basic education for poor people who were at work during the week. Naturally the heavy personal and financial investment of Christians in schools continued to shape the content of teaching and to make schools a major force in introducing a Christian content to the culture.

4.24 State responsibility for public education, and an explosion in human knowledge which has driven the content of the Christian tradition to the margins of the curriculum, have created a new situation with which the Church is still struggling. This development is both a cause and a result of the collapse of knowledge about the Christian belief and practice in the culture.

4.25 Deciding how to respond to this new situation has puzzled and divided Christians. The 1986 Education Act has led to many Church people having to put considerable energy into supporting schools. The 1988 Act's attempt to strengthen the Christian content of Religious Education may be undermined by the shortage of trained RE teachers. The commitment of Christians to local schools is likely to gain wide respect for the Church. In certain schools, where Church control is strong or able Christian teachers are involved, schools will still contribute to public understanding of Christian belief and practice. Despite this, many Church communities now question the priority of such demands. At the same time Church schools remain generally popular and oversubscribed.

4.26 However the Church at large needs to understand that schools on their own are not again going to be seen as an effective channel into Church life. Nor are they going to play any significant role in creating public understanding of the content or practice of the Christian way. However schools will continue to play a major role in defining the core beliefs and canon of knowledge in British culture. This has a number of implications:

Congregations and dioceses must take much greater responsibility for the formation of Christians.

Many adults become Christians in their 30s rather than their teens.[7] Reliance on school formation is not enough; resources must be made available for the Christian formation of adults. This last is already an area of growth and further developments are to be welcomed.

Cultural pluralism should not be seen as a threat; it can create space, in a somewhat alien culture, for the emergence of Christian communities which will, in turn, be places of education and have a role in forming the emerging culture.

Evangelism and Christian formation will need to make informed allowance for the way in which schools are shaping emerging English culture. This should involve sympathetic as well as critical evaluation. People who are undermined by their schooling must not be written off.

The new philosophy of partnership between educational institutions and the community needs to be welcomed and responded to.

A wider vision of education is needed in which personal formation and attaining wisdom are not seen as limited to schools or to adolescence. In this connection Christians should be sympathetic to, and get involved in, developing schools as community education resources.

Home-based formation

4.27 In Old Testament and Jewish culture the home or household is the primary place of spiritual formation. It is a place for instruction and reflection (cf. Deut. 6.4-9). Institutions such as the sabbath and Passover make the home a prime locus for worship that in turn becomes an important occasion for instruction, discussion and learning (cf Ex. 13.8,14; 20.9). Adults as well as children are the subjects of this activity.

4.28 The modern situation is much more complex; some of this complexity has to be understood if unrealistic expectations are to be avoided and parents within, and on the margins of, Church life preserved from unnecessary guilt.

4.29 Christians do not share the theological basis for this important feature of Jewish practice: membership of the people of God does not rest on familial inheritance (John 1.12,13; cf Luke 3.8; Rom. 9.8; Gal. 3.6,7). (People, even young people, often come to faith quite apart from the faith commitment of their natural family.) Jesus's institution of the eucharist takes a domestic rite and adapts it as the focus of the non-familial 'household of God'. The New Testament warns that the claims of Christ can disrupt family cohesion (Luke 12.49-53). At the same time it treats children as members of the household of faith and there is an assumption that prayer and learning will be part of the fabric of ordinary domestic life.

4.30 Furthermore the home should not be seen in isolation. Since the industrial revolution the home has tended to be seen as a place of refuge from wider society rather than an integral element within the whole social order. This has increased the pressures and expectations of domestic life while obscuring the links between it and wider society. The home is not the only place of personal and religious formation. Young people are formed by influences outside the home and are preparing for life in wider society. Both the civil community and the wider Church also have a responsibility for the nurture of young people.

4.31 Many parents are creative in finding ways of weaving Christian faith into the shifting patterns of their domestic life. Fine resources are made available by various organisations and publishers which can transform prayer and Christian formation in the home. Changing social conditions have inevitably affected the traditions of family prayer. Some activities can be based on well-established traditions; others can be totally unique to individual families.[8] Where practical the experience of regular individual and family prayer, worship and Bible reading can be introduced.

4.32 Various factors, including Jewish models, have brought a new appreciation of domestic prayer based on meals and on natural moments of celebration or reflection. The inclusion of prayers, including table graces, under 'For Church and Home' in *The Promise of His Glory* (pp.136-144) is a welcome development that perhaps needs to be taken further. There would be obvious gains in establishing links between domestic prayer and public liturgy. The Jewish insight that domestic prayer and celebration is not simply 'for the children' has probably yet to be assimilated.

4.33 The area of domestic prayer and instruction is one that needs to be identified and fostered and should figure in parish and national approaches to Christian formation. Account needs to be taken of the uncertainty and difficulties felt by people on the margins of church life. Very welcome is the development of approaches to help people become more aware and self-confident in their parenting skills. A course pioneered through Catholic schools and parishes is already being used in some Church of England dioceses, parishes and schools.[9] Some of the material available for the follow up of baptism families gives brief but practical help to parents, both in day to day relationships and behaviour, as well in encouraging their child's spiritual understanding and development.[10] The Southwark Diocesan Board of Education have produced a booklet *Caught and Taught* to provide ideas and encouragement in this area. Most Sunday School material includes work to be followed up at home. CPAS have published a video based training course *Help! I'm a parent.*

Church-based learning

4.34 In the future much Christian learning must be based in congregations. This will require conscious attention to learning processes as well as to the structuring and resourcing of Church life, both in congregations and in a wider context. Much wisdom is to be found in a fine series of Church reports produced in recent years,[11] many of them ecumenical. The subject is a vast one but a number of issues or principles can be identified as relevant as the Church assimilates a catechumenal approach to initiation:

Christian formation should not be limited to initial formation.

Theories of adult learning and faith development need to be respected and evaluated. Careful attention needs to be given to models of faith development such as Westerhoff's four styles of faith (experienced, affiliative, searching and owned) that explore the way in which the faith of both adults and children grows.

There needs to be an open and dynamic relationship with other places of learning in the community.

There needs to be a willingness to think and act ecumenically.

There needs to be a healthy and open relationship with denominational and interdenominational organisations and with Christian publishers.

Successful models of groups learning together keep a good balance between study and sharing of personal experience, individual and group activity, input and discussion, worship/prayer and social activity.

Learning works best when the content is owned by the group.

People's experience of God needs to be expected and respected.

Christian learning should involve memory and information as well as reflection and relationship.

Knowledge and love of the scriptures needs to be expected and encouraged.

Learning brings pleasure and growth; it also involves work, pain, change and openness to new ideas.

Education that does not maintain space for unwelcome questions and perspectives fails both individual and Church.

Christian formation involves apprenticeship within the Christian community: relationship, imitation, reflection, action and study.

The experience of accompanying enquirers on their journey of faith should stimulate the desire to learn.

The growing recognition of the role of the laity in leading 'enquirers' or nurture groups needs to be matched by a recognition of the importance of training and preparation, and of providing proper support structures at parish, deanery or diocesan level.

Diocesan, national and ecumenical support agencies may be required. Regional co-ordination of educational resources might help if constraints of money and personel could be overcome.

> *Increasingly baptism is seen as a sacrament of significance in its own right that points Christians to their true identity, character and calling.*

> *RITE.   Sacramental celebration must be*
> *prayerful*
> *confident*
> *generous*
> *corporate*
> *leisurely*

The recovery of rite

4.35 Until recently ritual has had a negative press in English culture, with certain national pageants being an honourable exception. Serious religion was thought to be concerned with motive and morals. Against the evidence of history the Pharisees were pilloried as ritual formalists. The common English complaint that Church people are hypocrites reflects the same hostility to ritual activity. Even the early Tractarians were suspicious of the Oxford Movement's interest in ritual reform.

4.36 There are many signs that things are changing. The discipline of social anthropology has shown that ritual behaviour is all pervasive and an essential element of social structure and interaction. Rituals are all around us and integral to the affirmation of personal identity and to the personal and social negotiation of change. In many areas of life the place of rite is being respected and reaffirmed. One example is the new emphasis on funerals for stillborn children. Another is a new recognition of the importance of ritual in pastoral care.[12] Many aspects of contemporary culture are now more hospitable to imaginative ritual and celebration in ordinary life. Many younger people are at home with styles of celebration which earlier generations might have dismissed as primitive. Many people are increasingly at home with symbolic modes of action.

4.37 Rite has a part to play in affirming personal identity and in marking and managing change. The generous but natural use of ritual is an important part of the life and ministry of the Church.

The problem of strangeness

4.38 Many people with a concern for evangelism are sharply aware of how bewildering many aspects of Church life are to those outside its life. A common response proposes the abandonment of alien elements in order to make worship more accessible. Such a response often focuses on such matters as styles of music or liturgical dress. However the problem runs much deeper. The simple actions of singing together, listening to the public reading of scripture, or sharing in communion do not relate easily to ordinary forms of social behaviour. Many people lack any experience of participating in a group as large as a congregation. Clergy sometimes comment on non-churchgoers' lack of comprehension of basic biblical or doctrinal material in the marriage and funeral rites and occasionally suggest that these rites should be simplified by eliminating biblical material and any difficult ideas or unfamiliar terms.

4.39 Those who make such comments perhaps need to recognise that Christian practice is shaped by stories or perceptions that are integral to the Christian way, even if they are now perceived as alien. One of the main ways in which the presence and character of an alternative way is made visible in the culture is by their embodiment in the public rites of the Church. Although this can be daunting it is an important part in mature Christian formation. The Church is not the only group or activity in the culture which has to make itself visible to those who have little initial comprehension of what it is about. The problem is made more severe by the absence of a bridging environment in which people can explore and assimilate the patterns of Christian worship.

4.40 This is not to suggest that liturgical practice does not need to take contemporary cultures seriously. It is however important to establish a two-way traffic; those to whom Church life is alien need a context in which they can come to understand the forms and roots of Christian practice: those who are at home within Church cultures need a place to reflect on possible challenges from the society around. It is one of the potential strengths of catechumenal approaches that they create a realistic context in which such mutual learning can occur.

The rediscovery of baptism

4.41 Over the last hundred years Christians have been involved in the rediscovery of the meaning of baptism. Prior to this, baptism was often treated as a sort of natural birth rite in a Christian society. Where there was controversy it often reflected other anxieties – such as the nature of salvation, the importance of personal faith, or a desire to clarify the boundaries of the Church in a more sceptical culture – rather than an appreciation of the theological importance of baptism itself. Various factors have contributed to a revival of baptismal theology: overseas mission, patristic and biblical study, the changing social context of the Church.

4.42 The 1982 Lima document *Baptism, Eucharist and Ministry* shows that baptism continues to be an area of controversy and division but provides eloquent testimony to the theological richness that the Churches are now finding in this sacrament. There was a tendency to see baptism as an isolated moment in the Christian life and as the gateway to the eucharist, the one proper sacramental focus of the Christian life. Increasingly baptism is seen as a sacrament of significance in its own right that points Christians to their true identity, character and calling. St Paul repeatedly refers his hearers back to baptism not simply as a reminder of their conversion but as a way of bringing home to them what it is to be in Christ.

4.43 In 1891 A.J. Mason could write 'the main difficulty lies less in defining what confirmation adds to baptism, than in defining what baptism confers apart from confirmation'.[13] The comment shows a lack of focus on baptismal theology with which few people could identify today. The point has already been made that liturgical provision needs to make the baptismal roots of Christian life more explicit. Although it is important to provide people with opportunities to renew their commitment to Christ, it is equally important to reaffirm the grace and promise of God inherent in baptism. The recent practice of highlighting 'the renewal of baptismal vows' does not always maintain this balance.

The question of confirmation

4.44 Although there have been more than a hundred years of discussion and controversy about confirmation, some of the basic historical background to the 'traditional' Anglican pattern is only now beginning to become widely known. It is still something of a surprise to many Anglicans that neither the ancient Church nor the Orthodox know a rite separated from baptism that carries the expectations associated in Anglican practice with confirmation. Commonplaces of liturgical scholarship are still unfamiliar to many who are called upon to consider contemporary practice. Examples are: the late and slow development of a separate episcopal rite in the West; the fact of eucharistic communion from infancy in the early centuries; the drastic decline in lay reception of communion from the fourth century;[14] the withdrawal of the bread from children in the eleventh century as a byproduct of controversy about eucharistic presence;[15] the withdrawal of the chalice from all the laity in the thirteenth century,[16] the thirteenth-century attempt to revive confirmation by making it the normal preliminary to communion;[17] Archbishop Cranmer's strategic innovation of linking the rite with catechesis. Less well known – but radical in its implications – is the realisation that episcopal laying on of hands was probably not linked with prayer for the Holy Spirit in the earliest Western tradition.[18]

4.45 This is not to imply that developments from early ideas and practice are necessarily illegitimate. There are many areas of Church life and theology in which later developments are viewed as significant gains. In many ways the controversies that have surrounded confirmation arise because of the accumulation of important theological and pastoral themes or concerns that this rite has attracted to itself. One of the difficulties that stands in the way of recognising new patterns is a legitimate anxiety that an undermining of recent Anglican pastoral practice will leave very important theological or pastoral themes with no definite locus in the life of the Church. For an alternative initiatory framework to gain assent, these anxieties must be addressed.

4.46 One of the major trends in Church life between 1850 and 1970 was a new focusing on the idea of confirmation. After the Reformation the rite of confirmation signified primarily adult commitment and allegiance to episcopal order. In the nineteenth century the pastoral revival of confirmation by evangelical and tractarian bishops was followed by a revival of theological interest in confirmation. This led in turn to the formulation of a particular 'two stage' theology, with baptism and confirmation seen as two parts of the one sacrament of initiation, that has not stood the test of time. It was unfortunate that these pastoral and theological developments took place against an inadequate theology of baptism. The teaching and practice of this era are characterised by three important intertwined motifs: the Spirit, catholicity and commitment.

4.47 Anglicanism was not alone in this new interest in confirmation. For example, the term confirmation came to new prominence in the reunited

Church of Scotland with its 1940 *Book of Common Order* where it caused controversy by its use in the 'The Order for the Confirmation of Baptised Persons and for Their Admission to the Lord's Supper'. The opening address in this rite spoke of 'the Confirmation of their Baptism'; the word 'confirm' also occurs later in the rite in a prayer of blessing based on 1 Thess. 3.13. Again in 1962 the British Methodist tradition decided to adopt the term as an alternative title to its Order for Public Reception into Full Membership, a decision reflected in subsequent liturgical books. In some, but not all, of these Protestant traditions, these rites add a further idea in that they also signify responsible membership of a church or congregation. The 1980 and 1989 Service Books of the United Reformed Church, which are not mandatory in that tradition, use the term confirmation for a laying on of hands with prayer that precedes – and perhaps implies – welcome into a Church membership that is both universal and congregational.

4.48 When the various rites and traditions are examined in detail it emerges that the word confirmation is used to signify different aspects of the initiatory process as well as different liturgical elements of the rite. In early Western practice the word *confirmare* meant 'establish' or 'secure' rather than 'strengthen' and refers to the action of the Church not the candidate. It was a non-technical term that could be applied to the communion of the newly baptised or to the post-baptismal anointing and laying on of hands by the bishop. It only emerged as the technical term for the episcopal rite in the ninth century.[19] Even then it has continued to change and gain meanings. In the thirteenth century the sense of strength to bear witness and resist temptation became widespread.[20] With the 1662 Book of Common Prayer the further meaning of individual ratification of baptismal commitment became established.

4.49 Not only is the term confirmation used of different aspects of the initiation process. There has been disagreement about which part of the rite constitutes confirmation. Thus Western catholic thought has disagreed as to whether the essential act was the stretching out of the bishop's hands during the prayer for the seven-fold gift of the Spirit or the individual laying on of hands (or chrismation) that follows it. For Roman Catholics the matter has been settled by Pope Paul VI who declared in 1971 that it is the second act towards the individual that constitutes confirmation.[21] To complicate matters further, the RCIA permits Roman Catholic bishops to delegate confirmation (with episcopally consecrated chrism) to presbyters; the main reason for this is to enable adults and older children to receive baptism and communion in one service.

4.50 The often quoted description of confirmation as 'a rite in search of a theology' does not do justice to the situation we have attempted to sketch. The reality is that many important aspects of the process of Christian initiation have come to be focused on one episcopal rite, drawing strength from this complex history and the multiple meanings of the word confirmation – and often drawing attention away from the sacrament of baptism, the true focus of Christian initiation. The difficulty is not a lack of theology but the over-concentration of too much theology on one moment in the process.

4.51 The concentration of so much theology on one episcopal rite of laying on of hands not only distorts the pastoral process, it also tends to skew theological perceptions of initiation. One example is the common Western mistake of viewing chrismation in the Orthodox and Syrian tradition as simply an Eastern version of Western confirmation with little sensitivity to other traditions' rich appropriation of baptismal themes.[22] Another example occurs in the use of confirmation to receive members of other Churches into communion in the Church of England. This has the effect of linking too closely commitment within our episcopally ordered Church with inappropriate suggestions of an initial commitment to Christ or some implied deficit in the Holy Spirit's presence in non-episcopal Churches.

4.52 A further result of this concentration of theological expectations on the one rite of confirmation is the difficulty of distinguishing those aspects which are unrepeatable because of their link with baptism and those which are intrinsically repeatable as ways of appropriating baptismal grace. The ancient Church used the laying on of hands not only to pray for the newly baptised but also to reconcile penitents and heretics.[23] Without encouraging excessive ritualisation there are often good pastoral reasons why someone should make a new public affirmation of the Christian faith or should receive prayer focused by the bishop's laying on of hands.

4.53 The July 1991 General Synod Motion asked the Liturgical Commission 'to prepare a series of rites described as Route Three in GS Misc 366 for the renewal of baptismal vows, for the reception of members of another Church, and for reconciliation and healing'. The proposals embodied in this motion are described by David Stancliffe and Kenneth

Stevenson in the paper referred to as representing 'a renewed and extended view of Confirmation, akin to the Pastoral Offices, in which the bishop's role is the norm'.[24]

4.54 This notion of extended or stretched confirmation has the great merit of acknowledging the important and potent themes associated with confirmation while addressing their over-concentration in one single rite. It fits well with the attempt of catechumenate approaches to acknowledge the process character of initiation and can be seen as a further example of identifying and redistributing aspects of initiation. This approach has been adopted by the Episcopal Church in the USA whose 1979 *Book of Common Prayer* places confirmation, reaffirmation and reception under Pastoral Offices. This has been carried through into their Canon Law which treats this episcopal reception as canonically equivalent to confirmation. A similar approach is indicated in the Anglican Church in Canada's 1985 *Book of Alternative Services* which places confirmation, reaffirmation and reception under Episcopal Offices.

4.55 It is important to note that this represents a different approach to one which has been favoured in certain circles and can be summarised in the phrase, 'reintegrating the fragmented rite of Christian Initiation'. Where this was seen as implying that there was an original single rite comprising baptism-confirmation-communion, this assumption has been called in question by the study of patristic liturgical practice. However the difference between the two approaches is probably more a matter of terms than substance. It is common ground to both positions that prayer for the gift of the Spirit is an important part of any baptismal rite. Equally both views wish to guard the role of the bishop in initiation. However, in the approach adopted by Anglicans in USA, New Zealand and Canada (and which underlie GS Misc 366), the actual term 'confirmation' is allowed to gravitate to the post-baptismal context which the pastoral tradition of recent centuries has made familiar.

4.56 The practice of requiring confirmation of non-Anglicans has been a source of controversy, even embarrassment, for some time. The assumption in Canon B15A that 'the normal requirement' for communicant status in the Church of England is episcopal confirmation has been used to require the confirmation (often re-confirmation) of people from non-episcopal Churches while other forms of reception have been adopted for Roman Catholics and Orthodox. In the case of the

Orthodox this has involved a Western reading of the Orthodox practice of chrismation. A further complication is arising with the advent of presbyteral confirmation in the Roman Catholic Church.

4.57 A new dimension is created by the proposed Porvoo Declaration,[25] resulting from conversations with Nordic and Baltic Lutheran Churches that are episcopally ordered but practise presbyteral confirmation without the use of chrism. The Bishop of Grimsby, as co-chairman of the Conversations that led to the Declaration, has suggested that after the Declaration has been approved,

> the Church of England may be willing to consider legislation to provide that references to confirmation should be interpreted as meaning either confirmation by a bishop or confirmation by a priest in an episcopally ordered Church in communion with the Church of England.[26]

4.58 The adoption of the rites which the Liturgical Commission has been asked to prepare will require some change in the current practice for admission to Communion. The mechanism for such changes exists through the adoption by Synod of regulations as envisaged in Canon B.15A (see Appendix 5). The broadening envisaged by the Porvoo Declaration could also be achieved by this mechanism.

4.59 The adoption of a catechumenal framework for Christian initiation in the Church of England would not necessarily require any change to the current canonical provisions. However it will be important that suitable rites are available for those who have been baptised (and perhaps confirmed) and subsequently enrol as enquirers. Such rites will not only have to bear the weight required of them as the climax to an extended process, it will also be important that they help the individual to a fuller appreciation of their baptism.

4.60 At the same time the coherence and clarity of the framework may be increased if certain alternative patterns are permitted. The Group's main suggestions are set out in chapter 6. In chapter 7 some of the implications of these proposals are explored. In particular, consideration is given as to where the various concerns currently focused on confirmation are to be located. In this connection possible consequent changes are suggested.

4 – Ethics

The intention of the New Testament writers was not to develop a coherent form of moral discourse but to root communities and individuals in their baptismal character and calling and to enable them to reflect and serve the kingdom of God. New Testament ethics are rooted in baptism and mission.

4.61 'Put to death therefore what is earthly in you: ... Do not lie to one another, seeing that you have put off the old nature [humanity] with its practices and have put on the new nature [humanity], which is being renewed in knowledge after the image of its creator.'(Col. 3.5,9,10). New Testament ethical exhortation is firmly rooted in baptism, and in the complex images of redemption and new creation associated with baptism.

4.62 The explicit ethical exhortations which often occur in the second part of New Testament letters assume the new social reality of the Church. They are carefully framed to link their instruction with the richness of the gospel and with the new creation established in Christ. Their concern is to establish patterns of thought, character, relationship and behaviour and to relate these to the new order made manifest in the gospel. Particular ethical material often arose from the social context in which the Church found itself and drew on traditions of ethical instruction already well established in the culture. The purpose of such instruction was not simply moral; it was to root the Churches more deeply in Christ. It does not treat the Christian life as an isolated end in itself; it is framed within a broader social context with the intention of confirming the Church in its commitment to God's mission in the world.

4.63 The significance of ethical material in the New Testament often lies not in its specific content but in its broader theological and social context. The intention of the writers was not to develop a coherent form of moral discourse but to root communities and individuals in their baptismal character and calling and to enable them to reflect and serve the kingdom of God. New Testament ethics are rooted in baptism and mission.

4.64 The Didache, one of the earliest of post-New Testament documents, frames its baptismal instruction around the idea of the Way. This had the advantage of picking up a scriptural image, of relating baptismal catechesis to broader traditions of ethical teaching, and of confirming the integration and patterning of Christian believing and living.

4.65 It would be impossible to summarise the subsequent history of Christian ethical thought. As the social context of the Church changed it naturally became preoccupied with different issues and perspectives. Particular moments in this developing tradition continue to exercise a potent influence. Augustine's brilliant use of the biblical images of Babylon and Jerusalem has had a lasting influence on political thought. The scholastic analysis of moral action in matters such as war and economics remain an important, if neglected, resource. The Reformers focused their concern to provide a shape to Christian life in the world in systematic exposition of the Ten Commandments, thereby giving this text an important status in Protestant and Anglican thought. Each of these developments can be seen as expressing the link between Christian ethics and God's mission in history. The links between Christian ethics and baptism, however, have tended to be overshadowed.

4.66 In recent centuries Western ethical theories have often been preoccupied with the basis of the human moral sense, with the resolution of difficult moral dilemmas, and more lately with issues raised by cultural relativity. In the last two decades writers on ethics, represented for example by Alasdair MacIntyre with his book *After Virtue* (1981), have attempted to shift the focus to the ethos that underpins particular moral action and to emphasise the role of community ethos and the establishment of the habits and patterns we call character. A similar shift is occurring in Christian ethical thinking with, for example, Oliver O'Donovan[27] exploring the theological roots, and Stanley Hauerwas[28] concentrating more on the ecclesial context of Christian approaches to ethics.

4.67 These developments throw a helpful light on the priorities in the ethical formation of new Christians. The patterning of Christian ethical response is a very important part of the initiation of new Christians. A number of recent contributions by Anglican thinkers have highlighted the role of liturgical forms in patterning Christian ethical thinking and social response. Rowan Williams has described the particular concern of the Book of Common Prayer to equip and inform a broad Christian vision in its particular social context.[29] John Gladwin has identified the need to explore and re-express in contemporary liturgical provision the inclusive social vision underlying the Book of Common Prayer and the approach of Anglicans such as Hooker.[30] Oliver O'Donovan has emphasised the role liturgical forms play in providing Christians with basic moral categories, an overall moral vision, and perspectives for interpreting the world.[31]

4.68　These perspectives point to three important issues for the initiation and formation of new Christians:

i.　The role of liturgy in the ethical formation of Christians needs to be recognised. As has been noted this perpective needs to inform the drafting of liturgical material. It also means that forms of Christian initation that do not introduce people to the liturgical tradition risk deforming their ethical formation. People needed to be helped into the Church's liturgical practice in a way that gives them a grasp of their baptismal character and calling and directs their eyes to the society in which God has set them.

ii.　Part of ethical formation is gaining a sense of the shape of our ethical response to God. An important way in which this happens is the highlighting of certain central biblical texts both in public worship and personal formation. Oliver O'Donovan notes the distortion that arises if such texts are used in an exclusively penitential context.[32]

There are two texts which the Group believes need to be identified in this connection and to be used in the initial formation of Christians. The first is Jesus's summary of the law, with its dual focus on God and neighbour.　It is used in this way as early as the Didache and was restored to Anglican tradition under the influence of the non-Jurors.[33] The second is the Beatitudes which are used in the Orthodox tradition, and whose adoption is suggested by Rowan Williams as 'part of the evocation of the life of the Kingdom'.[34]

The use of the Ten Commandments is somewhat more problematic. Two difficulties arise. The first is a loss of confidence in how Christians are to use the ethical material of the Old Testament; there is a need to recover at a popular level the helpful traditions of Christian interpretation of this material.[35] The ASB's handling of the Commandments (Rite A, #78A) is particularly fine in this regard – and works best with one voice reading the Old Testament text and another the rest. The fact that it is rarely used points to the other difficulty with this text, namely its length. It is likely to be taken up in some contexts but it is difficult to see it being given the same profile as the first two.

iii. Great care needs to be taken over the handling of particular moral issues that may arise during initiation. Priority needs to be given to helping people gain a sense of the shape of the Christian response to God. The gospel is about freedom in Christ, a concept itself that needs to be affirmed and explored during initial formation. A catechetical process that fails to respect the conscience of individuals or attempts an over-rigid moral formation risks damaging the individual. It also risks making the Church culturally and socially monochrome; one of the potential strengths of catechumenal approaches lies precisely in its capacity to help the Church respect the diversity and particularity of those coming to faith.

Notes

1. cf 'Jeremy Taylor's Merely Spiritual Power', Reginald Askew, *Ecclesiastical Law Journal* 1994, pp.156-165

2. cf. *Finding Faith Today*, pp.16-18.

3. Martin Hengel, *Judaism and Hellenism* (SCM, 1974), Vol 1, pp.65-83.

4. Cambridge History of the Bible vol 1, pp.63,64.

5. J Leclercq, *The Love of Learning and the Desire for God* (Fordham University Press, N.Y., 1982), pp.2,20,115.

6. cf *The Fourth R – the Durham Report on Religious Education* (National Society & SPCK 1970), pp.1-6

7. *Finding Faith Today*, p.25

8. e.g. Marjorie Freeman,*We Always Put a Candle in the Window* (CHP/NS, 1989).

9. Micky and Terri Quinn, *What Can a Parent Do?* (Family Caring Trust, 1986).

10. e.g. *One to Five*, produced by the Carlisle Mothers' Union.

11. *The Child in the Church* (BCC, 1976); *Understanding Christian Nurture* (BCC, 1981); *Children in the Way* (National Society/CHP, 1988); *How Faith Grows : Faith Development in Christian Education* ed. J. Astley (National Society/CHP, 1991); *All God's Children?* (National Society/CHP, 1991); *All are Called* (CHP, 1985); *Called to be Adult Disciples* (GS 794, 1987). Also *Learning for Life*, Yvonne Craig (SPCK, 1994).

12. *Ritual and Pastoral Care*, Elaine Ramshaw (Fortress Press, 1987).

13. *The Relation of Confirmation to Baptism* cf. 'The Theology of Adult Initiation in the Nineteenth and Twentieth Centuries', David M. Thompson in *Adult Initiation*, ed Donald A. Whitley, (Alcuin/GROW, 1989).

14. cf. J.G. Davies, 'The introduction of the Numinous into the Liturgy' in *Studia Liturgica* vol 8. 1971/2, pp.216ff.

15. J.D.C. Fisher, *Christian Initiation in the Medieval West* (Alcuin Club/SPCK, 1965) pp.101-4.

16. *Ibid* pp.104-7

17. *Ibid* pp.123/4.

18. cf Aidan Kavanagh, *Confirmation : Origins and Reform* (Pueblo, 1988); reviewed by Paul Turner with response by Aidan Kavanagh in 'The Origins of Confirmation : An analysis of Adian Kavanagh's hypothesis' *Worship* 65, 1991, pp.320-338.

19. J.D.C. Fisher p.148.

20. *Ibid* p.134

21. cf. Gerard Austin, *Anointing with the Spirit, The Rite of Confirmation* (Pueblo, 1985). pp.42-47.

22. cf Paul Bradshaw, *The Search for the Origins of Christian Worship* (SPCK, 1992), chapter 7. cf 'The Transition to a Post-Baptismal Anointing in the Antiochene Rite', Sebastian Brock in *The Sacrifice of Praise*, ed Bryan Spinks (Rome, 1981), pp.2215-225 and *The Holy Spirit in the Syrian Baptismal Tradition*, Sebastian Brock (Poona 1979).

23. cf *The Origins of the Roman Rite*, ed Gordon Jeanes (Alcuin/GROW, 1991), pp.118-19.

24. *Christian Initiation and its Relation to Some Pastoral Offices* : A paper prepared on behalf of the Liturgical Commission by Kenneth Stevenson and David Stancliffe, 1991, pp.6-8; *Theology* Vol XCIV 1991, pp.284 ff.

25. *Together in Mission and Ministry : The Porvoo Common Statement with Essays on Church and Ministry in Northern Europe* (GS 1083, 1993), pp.30-31.

26. See Appendix 4.

27. *Resurrection and Moral Order* (Leicester/Grand Rapids, 1986).

28. *The Peaceable Kingdom* 1983; cf. L. Gregory Jones *Transformed Judgement : Towards a Trinitarian Account of the Moral Life* (Notre Dame, 1990).

29. 'Imagining the Kingdom : some questions for Anglican worship today' in *The Identity of Anglican Worship*, ed Kenneth Stevenson and Bryan Spinks (Mowbray, 1991), pp.1-13.

30. 'The Liturgy in the Social Context' in *The Renewal of Common Prayer*, ed Michael Perham, (CHP/SPCK, 1993), pp.37-42.

31. *Liturgy and Ethics* (Grove, 1993).

32. *Ibid* p.9.

33. G.J. Cuming, *A History of Anglican Liturgy* (Second Edition 1982), p.141.

34. *Ibid* p.9.

35. cf *Resurrection and Moral Order*, pp.159-160.

Chapter 5

THE INITIATION OF CHILDREN

5.1   At the heart of this Report is the desire to assimilate lessons from models of Christian initiation based on an adult catechumenate. The Group has seen in such catechumenal approaches an important attempt to integrate the different aspects of the formation and incorporation of new Christians. It has been concerned to make suggestions about the welcome of enquirers and the Christian initiation of adults and older children within the Church of England. It has also been concerned to re-examine the liturgical and formational framework in which this growth to faith takes place. Christian initiation must involve change for the Church as well as the individual being initiated. Christian initiation must not be seen simply as making demands on those outside the Church; it is about how Church and individual together can receive the gift of new life within the kingdom of God.

5.2   This report should be seen as complementary to two major Church of England reports which were directly concerned with the faith of children and their place within the life of the church. *Children in the Way* (1988), a Report of the General Synod Board of Education, set out a fresh approach to the children who are part of the Church and whose presence needs to be affirmed and whose contribution needs to recognised and supported. *All God's Children?* (1991), a Report of the General Synod Board of Education and Board of Mission, looks at the Church's responsibility to the 86 per cent of the nation's children who have no contact with any Christian Church. No attempt is made here to cover again the vital issues dealt with in these reports. The welcome and nurture of new Christians, infant or adult, is one of the most important tasks that faces the Christian community. Our hope is that the three reports will be seen together, and will help the Church of England to have a coherent and confident approach to this God-given priority.

5.3   Many of the themes drawn out in *Children in the Way* and *All God's Children?* are identical with those which emerge in current thinking about the initiation of adults. These include:

- the need to recognise and respect the life experience and integrity of the individual in their journey in faith;

- the need to provide an environment in which they can explore not simply Christian teaching but the lived experience of the Christian faith;

- the need of the Church to see itself as a pilgrim people journeying with, supporting and welcoming the individual;

- the need to see growth in faith as a complex and developing human process;

- the need to integrate personal formation, incorporation into the Christian community, and sacramental initiation in such a way that both Church and individual are fully engaged.

5.4   Within this common thinking this Report now seeks to address two questions which were beyond the scope of the earlier reports and which arise from the attempt in catechumenate approaches to integrate sacramental initiation and personal formation. The first is to look at the sort of institutional framework within which the initiation of children and the support of their families takes place. The second is to examine how the particular provisions for the initiation and nurture of children fit into the wider practice of Christian initiation.

5.5   Addressing these questions will in turn bring into focus other questions. Are there conflicts between the baptism of infants and the adoption of a catechumenal approach to adult initiation? Is the integrated framework inherited from the Reformation still adequate for the initiation and nurture of children in the Church? How should the Church handle requests from non-churchgoing parents for their children's baptism? These are matters about which there can be sharp controversy: evidence of the importance and difficulty of the issues with which the Church has to wrestle. In attempting to address them the concern of the Group has been to take seriously the strength and variety of current pastoral practice and to work toward a coherent framework for initiation in the Church of England.

Possible Conflicts with Infant Baptism

5.6   It is often thought that there is a conflict between the revival of a catechumenal approach to Christian initiation and the practice of infant baptism. For example the Roman Catholic Church found it necessary in

1980 to issue an Instruction on Infant Baptism which vigorously counters the views of those who 'think it better to delay the baptism of children until the completion of a catechumenate of greater or lesser duration ... [or who] wish the celebration of the sacrament to be put off until such an age when an individual can make a personal commitment, perhaps even until the beginning of adult life'.[1]

5.7   This suspicion of a possible conflict between these two practices may rest on a number of different factors that need to identified and examined.

Some may believe that infants are not possible candidates for baptism or that no person should be baptised until they have made a personal profession of faith. This clearly runs against the historic position of the Church of England. In asserting that infants are proper candidates for baptism, Anglicans have traditionally appealed both to the general tenor of scripture and to the historic tradition of the Church.

This position cannot appeal to the principles of catechumenal initiation for its justification. Integral to the catechumenal approach is the principle that people should be welcomed and embraced by the Church in a way that respects and responds to their starting point. In the case of infants and those suffering severe mental handicap[2] this principle requires that no demand be made which the individual cannot reasonably meet. The principle points to a practice in which the Church welcomes the individual in baptism and accepts the responsibility of nurturing their faith in a way appropriate to their circumstances and capacity.

Some are concerned that those baptised in infancy are deprived of the dramatic personal and corporate experience of baptism. In essence this position is close to the first but gains plausibility from the absence of a vibrant baptismal theology in the Church. Where baptism is seen not simply as the first moment in the Christian life, but as a lifelong identity to be lived out with the people of God and reappropriated in daily discipleship, people's awareness of the call and promise of baptism will not depend on their memory of some dramatic moment in the past.

This particular concern highlights the need to re-establish a strong baptismal theology in the life and liturgical practice of the Church.

Others again note the contrast between the thorough and careful attention given to the Christian formation of the individual in the catechumenate with its frequent absence in infant baptism as commonly practised. Various aspects of initiation which are integral to catechumenate approaches may be largely or entirely absent:

> prayer;
>
> a rich and joyful celebration of the gospel embodied in baptism;
>
> an accessible and real introduction to the Christian Way, to the scriptures and Christian worship;
>
> the encouragement of a personal response to Christ;
>
> incorporation into the Christian community.

In this case the difficulty is real and may be particularly sharp where the child is in the care of parents who have no real wish for contact with the Christian community. It would, of course, not be reasonable to expect the same concentration and intensity as accompanies the later stages of an adult journey to faith. Children grow up gradually and their Christian nurture needs to respect the pace of their human growth. This matter often raises as many questions about the baptising Church as it does about those who bring a child for baptism. The baptismal practice of a Church needs to be judged in part by the answer it would give to an unchurched parent who said, 'This is who we are; this is our starting point. How will you meet and help us?'

5.8   The systematic and integrated approach to Christian initiation and formation in catechumenate approaches forms a very useful point of reference in reviewing the Church's practice in the response to infants brought to it for baptism.

Catechumenal Approaches to the Baptism of Children

5.9   As yet the attempts to apply catechumenate approaches to the initiation of children have been limited and tentative. However they are sufficient to indicate that this is likely to be a fruitful way forward in the future. Some of the more significant of these approaches are:

> The RCIA itself includes a simplified form of catechumenal process for 'children who have reached catechetical age'. It sets up a three-stage process. First of all children are welcomed as catechumens by 'an actively participating but small congregation, since the presence of a

large group might make the children uncomfortable'.[3] It is clear from the rite that this marks an initial decision for faith rather than mere enrolment as an enquirer. The next step involves penitential rites that prepare the children for the full initiation that follows. They are confirmed by the bishop or priest who presides at the baptism. The pastoral instructions that accompany the rite deal thoroughly with the need to take the child's perspectives into account. Experience and reflection on this approach to the initiation of young children is beginning to be available from the USA.[4]

ICEL, the international Roman Catholic Comission which prepared the English language edition of the RCIA, is now beginning a ten-year project to examine the practice of infant baptism. In 1993 it issued a consultation document as part of this process. The current edition of the Rite of Baptism of Children already explores ways of involving parents and sponsors in the rite – for example by joining in the signing the children with the cross. There is every indication that this process will attempt to apply some of the lessons learned from the RCIA to the rite for infants.

The Episcopal Church in the USA has published a framework for 'The Preparation of Parents and Godparents for the Baptism of Infants and Young Children'.[5] This aims for pastoral contact during pregnancy, including use of 'The Blessing of Parents at the Beginning of Pregnancy'. Parents and godparents ('at least one a member of the local community') meet with a catechist and others during the pregnancy and then after the birth up to the baptism. Emphasis is placed on balanced Christian formation as well as the potential of 'prayer and worship in the home'. The birth is celebrated with a service of 'Thanksgiving for the Birth or Adoption of a Child'. Under special circumstances the deferral of the child's baptism is allowed 'until the child is old enough to go through the catechumenate'. In such cases, 'The parents should receive ongoing support in the formation of the child.'

A similar approach is described by Gail Ramshaw-Schmidt[6] who carefully links her proposals with relevant biblical material and also provides rites appropriate to different pastoral situations that might arise such as stillbirth or miscarriage.

An account that relates more obviously to the usual English pastoral context is to be found in the essays published to accompany the 1991

Toronto Statement.[7] Written by Ronald Dowling, an Anglican priest in Australia, it identifies three principles which need to be embodied in current practice:

i. The sacraments are the celebration by, of and for the gathered Christian community.

ii. Preparation for parents and godparents of infants is essential.

iii. The responsibility for the entire baptismal process, including preparation, belongs to the whole Church.

The essay does not underestimate the difficulty of establishing some measure of attendance and preparation in the period running up to the baptism; it reflects the same sorts of struggles to change expectations that are familiar in the English context. One of the possibilities he mentions is the introduction of the parents and godparents to the congregation some Sundays before the baptism in a brief rite in which they accept the role of sponsor and the discipline of preparing for that role in the intervening weeks.

The author comments on this general approach,

> It may appear to some, that the above suggestions will create a very rigorist process of baptismal preparation. All this will depend on how the local congregation owns the process, and how lovingly members of the congregation enter into building relationships with those families who come seeking baptism for their children.

There is evidence that many Church of England parishes of different traditions are adopting practices which can be related to aspects of the catechumenal process. Examples of this include:

– care and expense being taken to welcome and affirm enquiring parents. Adaptation of the ASB to include the note of welcome;

– the involvement of lay people in welcoming and in baptismal preparation;

– the provision of supporters to provide prayer and help to parents;

– the provision of Parents' and Toddlers' groups to provide support and an accessible starting point for further exploration;

– the provision of help and material to encourage the personal formation of the child.

Particularly interesting are various signs of the adoption of some sort of staged baptismal rite. Common is the use of the ASB's service of Thanksgiving as a first stage for all couples rather than an alternative to baptism. Another practice is the holding of a brief prayer service a day or two before the baptism. This provides an opportunity to rehearse the baptism as well as space for quiet prayer for the child and the family.

The problems of reconciling the feelings of baptism parties and regular congregations at the ordinary Sunday liturgy are well-known. Some churches have begun to hold occasional Sunday liturgies devoted entirely to baptism; this allows the service to be carefully tailored to baptism families and supported by the congregation. Another practice is to return to Sunday afternoon baptism services, but with supporting members of the church present and the baptism itself followed up by a welcome to parents and infant at a subsequent Sunday service.

5.10 It is clear that these various approaches address some of the difficulties experienced in the current, and often more abrupt, practice of the baptism of infants. The Group believes that some provision along these lines would need to be included in any revision of the baptism services.

The Reformation Model Today

5.11 In chapter 1 we showed that the Anglican Reformers sought to establish an integrated approach to sacramental initiation, Christian instruction, and the incorporation of those baptised in infancy into Church and society. This model took the child as its typical candidate. The formal ordering of sacramental initiation, adopted as part of this integrated strategy, remains the basic framework into which the Church of England attempts to fit the very diverse experience of people coming to, or returning to, Christian faith. It may be thought that the model – and its sacramental framework – continues to be a valid starting point for the formation of children growing up in the Church today. However a number of factors have changed the context from that in which the Reformation model sought to operate.

5.12 The Reformation model saw society as one Christian household, ordering its life under Christ through a particular understanding of the Christian faith. Adolescent confirmation was therefore seen as a rite of passage into a new encounter with the Christian faith within both Church

81

and society. Adult society today tends to treat religion as a private affair and not part of the fabric of public discourse; this has often led to confirmation operating as a rite of passage from the Church. In this respect the cultural link between instruction and schooling has not been a helpful association: the Nordic Lutheran Churches, which still bring large numbers of adolescents to confirmation, see most of them leave the Church as they leave school. The Church needs to value forms of youth work that play a bridging role over this divide.

5.13 The Reformation model could assume an experience of belonging, and placed all its emphasis on the importance of instruction. In addition, at least in formal terms, it portrayed instruction as the reception of a tradition.

5.14 It is probable that recent practice was over-hasty in rejecting the traditional emphasis on learning important texts by heart. However there has now been a decisive shift in our view of how children and adults learn and how faith is formed. Particularly with children it is generally accepted that the experience of belonging and the encouragement to explore and question are the necessary context for further learning. The analysis of how faith develops associated with John Westerhoff is widely acknowledged as having considerable validity.[8] He sees 'experienced faith' as being the basis on which subsequent styles of faith are established.

5.15 In this respect these theories of Christian education and nurture are in harmony with major theological themes which some express through the idea of grace and others through the theology of covenant These doctrines assert that God takes the initiative towards us: Christian learning and growth arise as we discover and assimilate a love that already exists. This emphasis on the primacy of grace pervades many modern approaches to both children and adults. It underlies the idea of welcome in catechumenal approaches to adults (cf Rom. 15.7). It is seen by many as the key to the pastoral efficacy of infant baptism: children experience the grace of Christ and so learn faith.

5.16 Educational theory and theological insight therefore both point to belonging as the basis of learning. However it may have functioned in the sixteenth and seventeenth centuries this is not how the Reformation model is now seen. At two points this has led to a radical departure from the Reformation model. The first is in educational priority: Christians of all traditions know that they have to work hard to create an environment of welcome and belonging before they can begin to share the content of the Christian faith.

5.17 The second is in the area of sacramental practice. In a Church which has achieved the Reformers' ideal of a weekly communicant eucharist, the exclusion of baptised and believing children from communion has increasingly been perceived as intolerable; at a pastoral and formational level it runs against the insight that belonging is the basis for learning. It is well-known that this remains a difficult issue in the Church of England; it will be addressed again below. A decisive step was taken in 1974 when General Synod in its debates on the 1971 Ely Report[9] accepted 'the principle that full sacramental participation within the Church may precede a mature Profession of Faith'.[10] Although it has proved difficult to agree the framework within which this principle can operate, a disjunction between admission to communion and the transition to adult independence was accepted. Whichever way the Church of England resolves this matter it is clear that it will not remain with the Reformation model of an adolescent confirmation that admits to communion.

The Authority to Baptise

5.18 The pastoral difficulties created by unchurched families who seek baptism for their children without any apparent interest in other aspects of the faith are a well-known cause of controversy and division. The sense that some Anglican parishes or clergy are actually or effectively refusing baptism is a cause of scandal to many. Before the Report looks at this precise pastoral issue it may be helpful to look in more general terms at the basis of the Church's authority to baptise.

5.19 When the Church baptises it is not simply providing a service for all and sundry, or acting as a retail outlet obliged by law to sell its goods to any who come; it is acting as God's agent and sharing in his work of mission.

5.20 The commissioning of the disciples in John 20.19-23 finishes with Jesus's recognition of the Church's authority to remit or retain sins (20.23), an authority that is exercised – perhaps chiefly exercised – in the act of baptism. The context of these words throws important light on the nature and limits of this authority. The authority is exercised by a Church which is exposing itself to the crucified and risen Christ's proclamation of peace (19-21a). It is exercised by a Church which is accepting Christ's commission to share in the divine mission focused in Jesus' coming in solidarity with the world and its sinfulness (21b). Its exercise requires the love and discernment of the Holy Spirit (22). These insights point to important constraints on how the Church exercises its authority to baptise. Baptism cannot simply be administered or organised by objective rules or detached commitments of policy. The act of baptism requires of the Church a delight in the grace of God, a costly identification with God's mission, and a discerning openness to the Holy Spirit who is active beyond its borders bearing witness to Christ (John 3.8; 15.26,27;16.7-11). This does not mean that the Church cannot refuse baptism. It does mean that a person refused baptism can legitimately ask how the mind and love of Christ is expressed in the refusal.

Parental Faith and Pastoral Strategy

5.21 The issue of how the Church should best respond to non-churchgoing parents who request baptism for their children is a difficult and divisive one. In view of the depth of feeling to which this subject often gives rise it is important to recognise the depth of the dilemmas which the issue raises. It is also important to avoid overhasty assumptions about the pastoral practice of other clergy or parishes; there is consider-able evidence that the practice of both 'open' and 'principled' parishes is the subject of considerable caricature. There may be plenty of bad practice on both sides; the exchange of stock horror stories is unlikely to help constructive discussion.

5.22 This issue is not simply an English or an Anglican matter. It is a continuing issue in ecumenical discussion and this dimension needs to be recognised. The 1982 Lima document raises it in the following terms,

> In order to overcome their differences, believer baptists and those who practise infant baptism should reconsider certain aspects of their practices. The first may seek to express more visibly the fact that children are placed under the protection of God's grace. The latter must guard themselves against the practice of apparently indiscriminate baptism and take more seriously their responsibility for the nurture of baptized children to mature commitment to Christ. (para. 16)

5.23 Not everyone will be happy with the terminology adopted here but it articulates an issue that should not be avoided.

The clash of expectations

5.24 One of the main difficulties in implementing any pastoral approach to this issue is the severe clash of expectations that quickly arise between non-churchgoing parents and clergy or congregations. Parents may well be moved by little more than social convention or they may have profound but inarticulate feelings of their child's need of God's favour; they are likely to have very little sense of what may be expected or asked of them. Clergy and congregation are often sharply aware of the demands as well as joys of public Christian discipleship. The two groups have very different starting points and there is often, in the nature of things, too little time for the clash of expectations to be explored.

5.25 The expectations of non-churchgoing parents are not irrational nor without history. Very often they are based on inherited patterns which they have had little reason to question. There are three elements in the shaping of this common memory which need to be identified.

5.26 The first results from the creeping withdrawal of explicit Christian faith and reference from public life, the media and schools. In a sense this has taken both parents and Churches by surprise. A situation now exists where explicit discipleship is more sharply focused than before on the Sunday eucharistic community.

5.27 The second factor is a widespread sense among many English working class people that the Church of England did not belong to them and would not be willing to accept them as they are. This is well articulated by *All God's Children?* in its discussion of a Sunday School culture that has now largely passed away;

> The cross-cultural reach of the Sunday school was remarkable. Children of all social backgrounds encountered Christians and the Christian gospel. Working-class adults revealed that their attitude to Christ was *not* negative. Many of them genuinely wanted their children to be taught about Christ. There was and still remains a deep-seated social and cultural alienation from the churches on the part of many working-class people. At least Sunday school brought the gospel into that culture. Gerald Priestland, in his famous radio series 'Priestland's Progress', coined the term 'the great Church of the unchurched'. He drew attention to the large numbers of people who had a belief in God as seen in Christ, who prayed fairly frequently and believed that they should try to live in a 'Christian' way morally. For many such people joining a church could still be an act of class betrayal or at least irrelevant. (para. 1.26)

While it may be true that over 90 per cent 'graduated' out of organised religion at the end of a period in Sunday school, there is no proof that this was because they were rejecting belief in Christ. The fact was that they attended largely because of the requirements of national custom and they eventually left *for precisely the same reason.* (para. 1.28)

5.28 In many ways the Church now finds itself responding to the residual cultural echo of the situation described here. There may be less explicit Christian faith outside the Church than this picture implies, but the sense of alienation persists. At a local level it means that a parish baptism policy has to address this sense that 'you don't really want our sort here'. It also points to the important link between the national stance of the Church on social issues and baptismal policy in areas still affected by the residual myths of working-class cultures.

5.29 A third factor shaping common parental expectation is an unintended consequence of the Reformation model of initiation. The pattern adopted by the Reformers had the effect of confirming the separation of baptism from the eucharist in the common memory. By contrast with the practice in Orthodox countries there has been nothing that demonstrated to people at the baptism of their children that this was intended to begin a life within the Church and focused on the eucharist. Taken with the style of public worship, the subliminal message was, 'They have all they need; now they are your responsibility until they are old enough to understand.'

5.30 The factors that shape the expectations of unchurched parents have sometimes shaped the attitudes of regular congregations. However the dominant influences within Churches have tended to be a fuller and more corporate spirituality, sometimes tinged by routine as well as the considerable demands of sustaining congregational life and finance. The dominance of the picture of the Church as the body of Christ over the last thirty years has played an important part in strengthening congregational life; the absence of references to 'neighbour' in modern liturgical rites may have undermined an awareness of solidarity with the local community. A major factor which continues to shape Church expectations is the sense that baptism is primarily a matter between the clergy and the people concerned.

5.31 This analysis of the difficult clash between parents and the worshipping community points to three pastoral priorities:

(i)   encouraging the congregation to see itself as a baptised people committed to mission;

(ii)   respectful engagement with the starting point of unchurched parents; and

(iii)   the creation of space and an appropriate context in which genuine encounter and welcome can occur.

The place of parental faith

5.32   The Book of Common Prayer's *Ministration of the Publick Baptism of Infants* makes no explicit demands on the faith of parents. The rite assumes no prior process of instruction but is designed to instruct those present within the rite itself. The weight of responsibility for the infant is placed on the godparents who answer 'in the name of this Child'. The rite urges those present to believe that God will answer their prayer, and at the end spells out to the godparents the particular responsibilities that they have undertaken. The tradition of making a proxy profession of faith for those too young to answer for themselves is already found in the baptismal practice of the third century.[11]

5.33   The approach adopted in the ASB arises from the General Synod debates in February and July 1974 arising from the 1971 'Ely' Report and particularly from the resolution adopted on 22nd February 1974.[12] Where candidates are infants or young children the parents and godparents are asked to make the baptismal renunciations and profession of faith in their own name as well as that of the child (#47,53 cf #43). In addition the separate rite for the Baptism of Children begins with an examination of parents and godparents to establish that they are willing to support the child 'by your prayers, by your example and by your teaching?'(#42).

5.34   This usage in the ASB has been highly valued by many as affirming within the actual rite the responsibility of the parents for the Christian nurture of their child. It has also been subject to a series of severe criticisms. The first refers to the tone of the rite, to its absence of welcome and to its apparent failure to accept the goodwill of the parents at this moment.

5.35   A second criticism objects to the bracketing of the parents' and the infant's baptismal profession. A number of concerns coincide here. Some object that this has the effect of disguising the real commitment to Christ being made on behalf of the child in the act of baptism, a matter which stands out clearly in the Book of Common Prayer and the tradition that precedes it, and which is focused in the practice of proxy vows.[13] Others object to the requirement that parents should make a personal commitment of the seriousness of a baptismal commitment at this moment when the child, and not themselves, is the focus of the rite. Others again wish more explicit account to be taken of the possibility of there being only one parent, or only one parent wishing to support the baptism.

5.36 Clarity is needed about this requirement of parental faith. It is sometimes defended on pastoral, and sometimes on theological grounds. A theological defence of a requirement of parental faith immediately runs against the strong New Testament insistence that membership of the people of God is not a matter of blood or racial descent (cf John 1.12,13; cf Luke 3.8; Rom. 9.8; Gal. 3.6,7). Nor does it relate easily with the New Testament practice of household baptism where the household will have included slaves and clients as well as blood relatives. This theological defence gains some of its power from the important insight that baptism is an expression of God's covenantal grace, a point that has often been deployed to great effect in defending the practice of infant baptism against its detractors.[14] However, as Colin Buchanan has suggested, the move from the covenant idea to the notion that the children of believing parents are appropriate candidates for baptism is not strictly a theological deduction or requirement; Old Testament practice serves more as an inductive pointer towards the appropriateness of baptising infants.[15]

5.37 The basic case for the requirement of parental faith is pastoral and, as such, needs to be taken seriously by its detractors. It is effectively based on the pastoral judgement that, in this social context, the child's only chance of the meaningful Christian nurture implied by its baptism is the full involvment of a believing parent. It is not enough to reply in general terms that the child is baptised 'in the faith of the Church'; for this to mean anything it must be saying that the Church intends to take responsibility for the child and to provide it with the rounded Christian nurture implied by its baptism.

5.38 However the basic problem with this pastoral defence of a requirement of parental faith is that it does not take seriously the starting point of many parents, and therefore risks asking too much too soon and forcing people to make statements in the rite for which they are not yet ready. In their journey of faith many parents are nearer to being enquirers in the sense in which this Report uses the term. At the same time the Church's responsibility in baptism demands that its practice of baptism is clearly associated with a commitment to subsequent Christian nurture. It is therefore reasonable in the rite to give very clear indications that baptism must be the gateway to nurture and a real participation in the Christian community. It might also be wiser to recognise the starting point of many parents who bring children for baptism and invite them to enrol as enquirers who will seriously explore the Christian Way in ways appropriate to them.

Approaching a pastoral strategy

An appropriate pastoral strategy for responding to requests from unchurched parents will need to include a number of elements:

— a realism about its difficulty and a recognition of the long-term character of changing expectations inside and outside the Church;

— the preparation of the local congregation so that they own their responsibility in baptism, and are willing to be identified with God's gracious approach to families seeking baptism;

— exploring the possibility of co-operating with Churches in the area, Anglican and other, or of adopting a common policy;

— providing a personal and accessible welcome to those who enquire about baptism for their children;

— being willing to see in such requests for baptism a sign of God's presence and an early step in the journey of faith;

— providing a context in which the parents feel affirmed and supported and in which they can begin to explore the implications of Christian discipleship;

— exploring ways of staging the rite of baptism so that families and congregation are able to experience it as a celebration of Christ;

— to present baptism so that it is clear that growth in faith and participation in the life of the Church are integral to Christian initiation and not additions to it;

— openness to the possibility of inviting individuals or families to enrol as enquirers;

– providing support and help in the Christian nurture of children and a style of Church life in which the children will feel welcome and can grow in faith;

– being ready to respond in creative and supportive ways to other issues, such as marriage, that may arise through the enquiry.

An infant catechumenate?

5.40 The possibility of enrolling children as catechumens has sometimes been proposed as part of a pastoral response to unchurched families seeking baptism for their children. Neither the Episcopal Church nor the Roman Catholic Church see this as a way forward in such cases. The Roman Catholic *Instruction on Infant Baptism* states,

> ... the pastors should keep in contact with the parents so as to secure, if possible, the conditions required on their part for the celebration of the sacrament. If even this solution fails, it can be suggested, as a last recourse, that the child be enrolled in a catechumenate to be given when the child reaches school age. (para. 30)

> Enrolment for a future catechumenate should not be accompanied by a specially created rite which would easily be taken as an equivalent of the sacrament itself. It should also be clear that this enrolment is not admittance to the catechumenate and that the infants enrolled cannot be considered catechumens with all the prerogatives attached to such. They must be presented later on for a catechumenate suited to their age ... (para. 31)

5.41 The Group does not take the view that the Church of England should enrol infants as enquirers. For someone to be welcomed as an enquirer it needs to be clear that they seriously intend to explore the Christian Way. The better way would seem to be to offer parents the possibility of enrolling as enquirers.

The transition to adulthood

5.42 One of the strengths of the Reformation model was that it acknowledged the transition from childhood to adulthood, and attempted to integrate this potent moment in human experience with a reappropriation of the Christian faith. There is a clear danger that early communion – whether by allowing communion before confirmation or by lowering the age of confirmation – risks depriving young people growing up within the Church of any supportive acknowledgement of this moment.

5.43 Because baptism expresses both the promise and call of God to each individual it needs to be affirmed and appropriated at various stages in human life. This is not a matter of somehow completing sacramental initiation; it is a question of grasping the implications of baptism for human life. The transition to adulthood is one such moment. It is important for the Church as well as the individual that the transition to independence and responsibility that occurs around the age of sixteen is properly recognised and affirmed.

5.44 Church-based youth work, such as CYFA, often has an important part to play in providing a structure for teenagers to make it through the pre-adult years into ministry within the Church, particularly where prevailing styles of worship require some adjustment or church culture is felt to be alien. Members of youth groups often get confirmed together, a comment on peer pressure and on the need for mutual encouragement. Churches which confirm young people in their early teens need to provide structures in Church life which can give teenagers Christian roots during turbulent years. The attempt in catechumenal processes to find forms of Christian formation that respect human reality may be a useful model in addressing this important task.

5.45 Clause (d) of the July 1991 General Synod motion asked 'the Liturgical Commission to prepare a rite of Adult Commitment as stated in paragraph 134 of GS Misc 365;'. The section referred to in Martin Reardon's discussion paper *Christian Initiation – A Policy for the Church of England* reads,

> .... The Church of England should, under guidelines from the House of Bishops, permit at least one other pattern in addition to what has become traditional. I believe they should permit either the Eastern pattern ... or confirmation at a much earlier age than is at present usual in the Church of England... If, however, they permit one or other of these options, then provision should be made for a personal profession of faith and act of commitment at a later age, perhaps in conjunction with admission to the electoral roll in a rite in which the candidate is admitted to the full privileges and responsibilities of adult membership of the Christian community.

5.46 There may be problems in linking such a rite with the electoral roll or with attempting to give a restrictive definition to the notion of membership or adult membership in the Church of England. However the Group endorses the principle embodied in this motion and suggests:

1. Parishes (and other bodies such as schools) should be encouraged, under guidelines from the diocesan bishop, to mark the transition to adulthood of young people growing up within, and on the fringes of, the Church. Where appropriate there should be an annual occasion when young people at or above the age of 16 may celebrate their coming to adulthood and renew their baptismal commitment. Where the young people have not been confirmed, confirmation should form the focus of this celebration. Where they have been confirmed, its focus should be the reaffirmation of baptismal faith.

In the preparation for such an occasion the young people concerned should be encouraged to commit themselves to four aspects of the Christian way: worship with the Church, growth in personal prayer, listening to the scriptures, and service and witness in the world. Opportunity should be provided for them to explore the particular responsibilities of adult members within the life of the Christian community.

The nature of this occasion may sometimes be served best by making it an annual event in its own right, not necessarily associated with the baptism, confirmation or reaffirmation of people of other ages. There would then be opportunity for appropriate social activities to express its meaning for young people and parish. It could appropriately be linked with other significant moments in parish life.

2. The Liturgical Commission should include within its rites of baptism, confirmation, and reaffirmation liturgical texts which will embody for appropriate candidates the shape and responsibilities of adult Christian discipleship.

3. While such a celebration is a desirable acknowledgement of the transition to adult life, it must not be seen as a essential stage or rite through which every individual must pass, nor should it be made the precondition of participation in any aspect of the life of the church.

Children and Communion

5.47 The practice of infant baptism, baptismal theologies that emphasise grace or covenant, and contemporary educational theories, all point to the same conclusion: the experience of belonging is the basis for nurture and growth in the Christian life. These three influences have fuelled pressure in many Churches for admitting children to communion from a young age, if not from baptism itself.[16] As the discussion of confirmation in chapter 4 attempted to show, such a move would be consistent with Christian practice in the first millennium of the Church and with the continuing practice of the Orthodox. The Church of England conceded something close to the principle in the 1974 motion referred to in para. 5.17 above; it has found it difficult to find an acceptable way to act on it.

Perceived difficulties

5.48 Advocates for radical change sometimes appear to promote this as a simple issue. The admission of children to communion is not however a simple matter. The complexity in part arises because of the subtle interlocking of pastoral and theological ideals embodied in the present theoretical framework for initiation in the Church of England. At the same time there are many indications that this framework itself is in trouble and not able to address many of the situations in which people come to faith today.

5.49 There are a number of different objections to admitting children to communion before confirmation:

Some think that an assertion is being made that baptism is complete Christian initiation. This misunderstands the position being advocated. For example, the 1991 Toronto Consultation affirmed the statement 'Children and Communion' of the First Anglican Liturgical Consultation in 1985. Its first recommendation read, 'that since baptism is the sacramental sign of full incorporation into the church, all baptized persons be admitted to communion'. Catechumenal approaches emphasise the different dimensions of Christian initiation and rightly urge their more effective integration with sacramental practice. What is being asserted is that full sacramental initiation is the proper precondition for the nurture of children growing up in the life of the Church.

Some are concerned that communion from infancy will further complicate the difficulties that arise from widespread infant baptism that does not lead to Church-based Christian discipleship. The point has already been made that the current discipline of the Church of England gives non-churchgoing parents little evidence that baptism necessarily involves continuing fellowship (communion) in the life of the Church. Adoption of the patristic and Orthodox practice may be too radical a step; it would however serve as a vivid corrective to popular understandings that baptism does not imply life in the Church.

Some are concerned that the proper marking of entry into adult life with its responsibilities and challenges will be lost. The Group shares this concern and has formulated the proposals set out above to address it.

Some are concerned that the change will remove from Christian initiation the element of clear incorporation into an episcopally ordered Church. It is clear that this concern must be properly addressed.

Some are concerned that the Church of England, by tampering with confirmation, risks abandoning an essential element in the historic practice of Christian initiation. The discussion in chapter 4 on 'The Question of Confirmation' provides some background for this. Contemporary scholarship does not appear to confirm the 're-integration of the fragmented rite' view of confirmation.[17] The term 'confirmation' itself does not have a fixed or settled place in the Christian tradition. One of the great strengths of catechumenal approaches to Christian initiation is that they preserve in an integrated way aspects of initiation to which confirmation attempts to bear witness.

The current situation

5.50 Since 1971 a series of reports from Church of England working parties[18] and from the International Anglican Liturgical Consultations[19] have recommended the admission of children to communion before confirmation. The latest of these, the 1991 Toronto consultation, was attended by 63 people from 21 churches of the Anglican Communion; its unanimous affirmation of the first recommendation in the 1985 statement has already been quoted. The reference in this recommendation to 'all baptised persons' indicates a significant shift within this developing movement in Anglicanism: where once the emphasis was on the pastoral need of children, it has moved closer to the Orthodox understanding that baptism admits to the communion of the Spirit and therefore necessarily implies eucharistic communion.

5.51 Children are now officially admitted to communion before confirmation by Anglican Churches in New Zealand, the United States, Canada and South Africa. It is under active consideration in other Anglican provinces.

5.52 Similar moves towards early communion have been made in other Churches. In 1987 the Methodist Conference published Guidelines for local churches with the intention that they 'actively ... encourage the fuller participation of children in the Lord's Supper'.[20] A similar policy of local action is now established in the Church of Scotland. The United Reformed Church has published a document *Children in Communion?*, and local churches have been encouraged to experiment.

5.53 Perhaps the most awkward ecumenical result of moving towards communion before confirmation is potential conflict with the theory, but not the practice, of initiation in the Roman Catholic Church. Formally the Roman Catholic Church upholds the tradition that the normative order for sacramental initiation is baptism-confirmation-communion.[21] The 1983 Code of Canon Law gives national bishops' conferences power to determine the age of confirmation, subject to confirmation by Rome.[22] In reality communion before confirmation has been the usual practice since the eucharistic revival of Pope Pius X at the beginning of this century resulted in a return to frequent and early communion. Currently the practice varies in different dioceses in England and Wales. Thus Salford diocese encourages confirmation at 7 prior to first communion; Arundel and Brighton does not permit confirmation before children reach the age of 14.

5.54 The General Synod debate in July 1991 indicated sharp division over the question of admission to communion before confirmation. Following this debate research was commissioned from Culham College Institute to evaluate experiments with communion before confirmation in the dioceses of Manchester, Peterborough and Southwark.. A report was published in 1993 which summarises the results from 80 per cent of the parishes authorised to vary their practice.[23] This indicates that a very substantial majority of these parishes were 'convinced of the positive value of admitting children before Confirmation'. The report singles out a number of important issues that arise in pastoral experience. These include: the importance of planning in advance, of having an integrated view of initiation, of creating a child-friendly church, of involving the parents at every stage; the need for nationwide recognition so that children may continue to communicate if they move to another parish; the arbitrary nature of attempts to fix a starting age for communion. A shift has already been noted from a pastoral concern with the faith development of children to a theological emphasis, not dissimilar to

Orthodox understanding, that baptism admits to the communion of the Spirit and therefore implies eucharistic communion. A corollary of the experiments appears to be seeing the continuing rite of confirmation as an adult rite concerned with taking responsibility.

5.55 The Culham Institute's Report would appear to highlight the need also for a serious pastoral evaluation of the traditional pattern. It would be difficult to do, but it is virtually impossible to compare the effectiveness of one pattern with another without such information.

5.56 The July 1991 motion appears to establish that three patterns now co-exist in the Church of England:

the Reformation tradition of confirmation, as simultaneously the gateway to communion and to Christian adulthood;

confirmation of younger children as entry to communion, recognising that their entry into Christian adulthood will follow at a later stage;

admission of the baptised to communion with confirmation coming later as the gateway to Christian adulthood.

5.57 We hope that a wider appreciation of an integrated approach to the initiation and formation of Christians, such as is modelled in catechumenate approaches, may lead to a greater understanding and unity between different approaches in the Church of England. The issues which need to be addressed include whether :

(i) parishes should be designated according to which of the initiation patterns they are following;

(ii) candidates from different options should be confirmed at different services. This would enable the focal liturgy to be related coherently to the process of initiation and formation to which it belongs;

(iii) children admitted to communion under the third pattern should be issued with a diocesan certificate that makes it clear that they are communicants.

Notes

1. Catholic Truth Society Do 525. #2
2. cf 'Cognitive Faith and the Problem of Mental Handicap in Canon Law', John A Griffiths, *Essays in Canon Law,* ed Norman Doe (Wales, 1992), pp.89-109
3. RCIA. #250

4. *Issues in the Christian Initiation of Children : Catechesis and Liturgy*, ed Kathy Brown & Frank C. Sokol (Liturgical Training Publications, Chicago 1989).

5. *The Book of Occasional Services* (Second Edition, 1988), pp.155-158.

6. Gail Ramshaw-Schmidt 'Celebrating Baptism in Stages: A Proposal' in *Alternative Futures for Worship* vol.2 pp.137-156, ed Mark Searle, Collegeville, (Liturgical Press 1987)

7. 'Preparing Parents for Infant Baptism', Ronald L. Dowling, *Growing in Newness of Life*, ed David Holeton (Anglican Book Centre, Toronto, 1993), pp.94-102.

8. cf *Children in the Way*, pp.38-43, *All God's Children?*, pp.49-51.

9. *Christian Initiation : Birth and Growth in the Christian Society* (GS 30).

10. 22nd February 1974 cf discussion in 1976 *Report of Proceedings* pp.815-855.

11. cf. *Hippolytus : A Text for Students*, ed G.J. Cuming (Grove, 1976), p18.

12. cf *Supplement for 1973-4 to Recent Liturgical Revision in the Church of England*, Colin Buchanan 1974, pp.10-11.

13. cf *Infant Baptism and the Gospel*, Colin Buchanan (DLT, 1993), pp.70-72.

14. cf *Believing in Baptism*, Gordon Kuhrt (Mowbray, 1987).

15. *Infant Baptism and the Gospel*, pp.16, 17

16. cf. *Children and Holy Communion : An Ecumenical Consideration amongst Churches in Britain and Ireland* (BCC, 1989).

17. See p.81 *Liturgy for a New Century* (1991, SPCK/Alcuin Club).

18. *Christian Initiation : Birth and Growth in the Christian Society* (GS 30) 1971; *Communion Before Confirmation?* 1985

19. *Children and Communion* (Boston, 1985); *Walk in the Newness of Life* (Toronto, 1991).

20. *Children at Holy Communion : Guidelines* (Methodist Church Division of Education and Youth, 1987).

21. See *One in 200? Towards Catholic Orthodox Unity*, Paul McPartlan

22. Canon 891.

23. *Communion Before Confirmation* (Culham College Institute).

Chapter 6

THE WAY FORWARD

6.1   The Group believes that catechumenal approaches to Christian initiation provide a helpful vantage point for reviewing the initiation and formation of adults and children in the Church of England. Particular strengths of this approach include:

– Attempting to integrate personal formation, sacramental initiation, and incorporation into the life and mission of the Church.

– Recovering of the significance of baptism for the ongoing life, calling and mission of the Church.

– Emphasising that the Church has a vital role in the welcome and formation of new Christians.

– Realising that coming to faith is a journey in which the enquirer needs the prayer and support of Christians.

– Taking seriously the need to respect the starting point of an enquirer and to learn from those whom God is leading to faith.

– Making clear that initiation and formation involve experience and reflection as well as instruction.

– Identifying of four elements that should be part of Christian formation:

worship with the Church
growth in prayer
listening to the scriptures
service and witness in the community.

– Using progressive rites to help mark an individual's journey in faith and to enable the Church to support them in prayer.

Future Patterns of Christian Initiation

6.2   We do not propose a single elaborate series of stages and rites as set out in the Roman Catholic *Rite of Christian Initiation of Adults*. There are great strengths in the flexibility of current patterns of evangelism and initiation in the Church of England. The better way seems to be to affirm what is good in present practice, to recognise that the Church of England is in a learning process, and to identify ways in which present practice might be improved. Catechumenate models provide an important starting point in any re-evaluation of the practice of initiation and formation. The Group hopes that this report will prove useful in assisting such reassessment.

6.3   In addition to identifying suitable criteria for re-examining initiation practice, the Group suggests two measures which are aimed at facilitating the welcome and formation of those on a journey to faith:

i.   That the Church of England should give formal recognition to the status of 'enquirer'. An enquirer would be a person, baptised or unbaptised, who, with the prayers and support of the Church, enters into a public exploration of the Christian way.

ii.   That the Church of England should make available additional forms of prayer that could be used before and after baptism, confirmation, reaffirmation of faith, or reception into communion. The purpose of these forms would be to enable a local congregation to journey with candidates for one or other of these rites.

6.4   It is *not* intended that these two suggestions should result in imposing a rigid or uniform pattern on the welcome or support of children or adults. Both locally and nationally, patterns of initiation in the Church of England need to recognise the complexity of the inherited traditions which shape expectations within and outside the Church. They also need to do justice to people's many different starting points and personal journeys.

6.5   It is important however, both for the individual and the Church, that Christian initiation and formation take place within a clear framework. The national provision of adequate liturgical rites has an important part to play in this. Also important is the adoption of a coherent and integrated approach at diocesan and congregational level. We therefore suggest that parishes and congregations be encouraged, under guidelines from the bishop, to identify and, if necessary, strengthen, their pastoral strategy for the initiation and support of new Christians, both children and adult. Some guidelines towards diocesan and parish policies are to be found in chapter 8.

6.6   Christian initiation and formation is not simply a matter for the Church of England. Baptism itself bears witness to the wider unity of the Church. There is a strong case for all the Churches in a locality working out a common baptismal policy.[1] This is not simply a question of taking the ecumenical implications of baptism seriously. It also acknowledges the confusion and division to which unrelated baptismal policies can give rise. There are already areas where such a policy exists and is in turn related to a joint education policy and catechumenal programme. Such local co-operation may strengthen the effective witness of churches which are not strong enough to implement an adequate approach to initiation on their own.

6.7   The issues raised by catechumenal approaches need to be taken into account in every aspect of the Church's involvement in Christian formation. There is a continuing need for the creation of catechetical and pastoral training material. In large part this is best left to the usual creative processes of parishes and voluntary societies. Again the Group hopes that this report will prove a useful resource in giving shape to such initiatives.

6.8   The proposals set out in this chapter, as well as the discussion in earlier chapters, invite some further clarification of issues that are still unresolved in the Church of England. The proposals in this chapter do not depend on any particular resolution of these questions. They are discussed with further suggestions in chapter 7.

Additional Liturgical Provision

6.9   In view of the importance of liturgical rites in recognising and supporting the growth of the individual in faith the Liturgical Commission may consider providing:

1. *A rite of welcome for an enquirer.* The rite should take account of the baptismal status of the individual.

2. *Prayers for those exploring the Way.* These should include appropriate material for :

   – use in home groups
   – insertion in the intercessions at public worship
   – prayers for individuals at particular moments in the Sunday liturgy

3. *Rites to precede and follow public celebrations of baptism, confirmation, reaffirmation or reception.* The purpose of these is to provide, where desired, a framework for candidate and church to journey together in drawing out and owning the meaning of baptism. These rites might consist of:

a. a rite of call and response in which enquirers or others are accepted as candidates for baptism, confirmation, reaffirmation, or reception.

b. appropriate lections to be used on the Sundays around the celebration or reaffirmation of baptism.

c. Prayers for the period before the rite. These should be available for candidates' groups and also for public worship. The main themes of this period should be 'Turning and Seeing anew'.

d. Prayers for use by candidates' groups and in public worship for the period after the rite. The themes of these should be 'Reflecting and Setting out'. This provision might include appropriate liturgical material for a church to celebrate and reappropriate the baptismal call to mission towards the end of the baptismal period.

4. *Prayers for parents and families during pregnancy.*

5. *Prayers and rites to surround the baptism of infants* so as to help parents and congregation assimilate the call and promise of baptism. These might include:

a. a form for the welcome and support of parents and godparents preparing for a child's baptism

b. a pre-baptism prayer service

c. 'free standing' Sunday baptismal liturgy

d. rite of welcome and reception at the Sunday eucharist

e. resources for use after baptism such as: prayers for use in the home, prayers for use on the anniversary of a baptism, an order for an occasional service for those whose children have recently been baptised.

6. *Appropriate material, for use with the rites of confirmation or reaffirmation,* to acknowledge the transition into adulthood.

6.10 It will be important that, in preparing these liturgical texts, language and images are used which are appropriate to the stage of growth into Christian understanding and commitment, and which will enable an appropriate response from individuals at different stages in their journey to faith.

The Pattern of the Christian Way

6.11 An important part of Christian initiation is helping the individual to discover and own patterns of Christian faith and practice. Some ways in which this can be helped are:

1. The four elements of Christian formation highlighted by catechumenate approaches i.e.

> worship with the church
> growth in prayer
> listening to the scriptures
> service and witness in the community.

2. The use of certain basic texts in the process of formation. The Group suggests that these should be the Lord's Prayer, the Apostles' Creed, the Summary of the Law, and the Beatitudes.

3. Questions about the Christian life have an important part in the initiation rites of other Anglican provinces. We believe that one such form should be adopted in Church of England rites and be seen as an important resource in the Christian formation of adults. One suitable form could be the 'Affirmation of Commitment' authorised by General Synod in *Affirmations of Faith* (CHP 1994). Another might be an adaptation of the questions in *A New Zealand Prayer Book*

4. A personal Rule of Life is a helpful discipline which individuals should be helped to work out and adopt. Once adopted they should be encouraged to review this on a regular basis.

5. A 'knapsack' of liturgical and devotional material for individual use needs to be identified. This idea has been proposed by Alan Wilkinson of Portsmouth and is commended by the Liturgical Commission in The Renewal of Common Prayer.[2] The purpose of such a knapsack would be to provide the individual with a core of devotional material which could inform his or her private prayer, be available in time of need, and provide a link between personal devotion and the public prayer of the Church. Work on the production of such a 'knapsack' is in hand with the hope that it will be published in the near future. It will be important for its coherence with the worshipping practice of the Church that the content and form of such a resource should be agreed with the Liturgical Commission.

6. A new Catechism should be prepared. This needs to draw on the experience and needs of those coming to faith. The Group did not take the view that the New Revised Catechism would necessarily be the best starting point in such an endeavour. It would be better to continue the authorisation of the 1962 Revised Catechism for the time being, and to allow time for further consideration of the form of a catechism in the light of the Church's reception of this Report. There would need to be clarity about the purpose and use of such a catechism. It would be against the insights and strengths of catechumenal approaches if such a document overshadowed personal faith sharing and reflection and encounter with the scriptures. Such a document, if appropriate, should only be a supplementary resource in personal formation.

Notes
1. cf *Christian Initiation – A Policy for the Church of England,* Martin Reardon (CHP, 1991), p.42.
2. SPCK 1993, pp.89-90.

Chapter 7

ESTABLISHING THE FRAMEWORK

7.1   The purpose of this chapter is to examine the way in which the suggestions made hitherto in this Report might fit into and develop current practice.   It also identifies certain unresolved issues which may need to be addressed if this approach is to find its rightful place within the formal ordering of initiation in the Church of England, and indicates possible ways in which they could be addressed.

The Role of confirmation

THE TERM "CONFIRMATION"

1. In the earliest and non-technical sense of establishing or securing, the term confirmation used of an action in which the Church accepts and acts on baptism. Applied to first receiving of communion as well as to episcopal anointing and laying on of hands.

2. In the West in the ninth century, it emerges in the technical sense of a post-baptismal episcopal rite.

3. In the thirteenth century the sense of strengthening becomes widespread, having been applied earlier to an adult's need of strength to witness and to resist temptation, and then transferred to children as they approach adulthood.

7.2   Chapter 1 of this report shows that the pattern of catechesis and sacramental discipline adopted by the Church of England at the Reformation has given a very high symbolic status to confirmation. In chapter 4 we attempted a map of current understandings of confirmation, and noted the way in which important theological and pastoral aspects or dimensions of initiation have come to be focused in the Church of England on the rite of confirmation. We also observed that General Synod's recommendation that the Liturgical Commission prepare rites for reaffirmation of faith (the renewal of baptismal vows) and reception into communion begins to draw on the idea of 'extending' or 'stretching' confirmation. If new patterns are to be established in the Church of England it needs to be clear how the particular concerns or themes that Anglican history has attached to the sacramental rite of confirmation will be focused and reaffirmed in any emerging pattern.

7.3   In order to give some indication of how the Group sees these concerns being met and where these important aspects of Christian Initiation are to be focused and safeguarded we list five concerns or themes which have come to be focused on confirmation:

The acknowledgement of entry into adulthood with its dangers and responsibilities. The Group suggests that parishes (and other bodies such as schools) might be encouraged, under guidelines from the diocesan bishop, to mark the transition to adulthood of young people growing up within, and on the fringes of, the Church. The focus for this would be either confirmation or, where people were already confirmed, reaffirmation of baptismal faith.

The highlighting of individual faith – a faith that is instructed and is professed before the Christian fellowship and the world in which the Church is set. The Group does not take the view that the baptism of infants requires a public profession of faith before it can be recognised as true Christian baptism. However it is important that personal and public response to Christ be encouraged and celebrated in the life of the Church. How this is done depends less on particular liturgical provision than on the style of Church life. Developing ecumenical contact with Churches practising 'believers baptism' suggests that there be clear and unambiguous recognition of this aspect of Christian faith.

The order for the reaffirmation of baptismal faith (renewal of baptismal vows) being prepared by the Liturgical Commission will be an important additional opportunity for such acknowledgement. The proposed celebration of entry into adulthood will provide a significant moment for those growing up within the Church. An approach to initiation and formation that fully involves the local congregation will highlight the importance of personal faith.

The need to have a clear framework in which to follow up the results of a tradition of open infant baptism. Two issues make this an important matter. The first is a widespread sense that baptism need not necessarily involve active participation in the Christian fellowship.

105

The second is the problem the Reformation model has in functioning effectively in a radically different social context.

The central need here is to establish patterns of initiation which clearly link sacramental initiation, personal faith and incorporation into the Christian community. This is the heart of catechumenal approaches to initiation and many of the suggestions in this Report are designed to ensure its establishment.

The importance of prayer and the charisms of the Holy Spirit in the initiation of the Christian. This is a major theme of the baptismal rite. It needs to be expressed in any rite that reaffirms baptism and to be explored with candidates before or after their baptism, confirmation or reaffirmation of faith.

Responsible commitment to the life and mission of a local church. This is an understated theme in English Anglicanism. It does however form a major element in a number of Protestant Churches.

It is more difficult for the Church of England to speak in terms of local church membership given its assumption of access for every parishioner. However two emphases in catechumenate approaches to formation may make links with this theme: involvement of the congregation in initiation; commitment of the initiated person to service and witness with the people of God.

The Ministry of the Bishop in Initiation

7.4   One concern in catechumenal approaches to Christian initiation is to involve the bishop fully in the process of initiation. There are five aspects of the bishop's role in initiation.

The bishop's role requires the bishop, either himself or through others, to guide the Church in initiation:

    i.   *in focusing the mission and unity of the Church*

    ii.   *in teaching the faith*

    iii.   *in protecting and providing for the enquirer*

    iv.   *in affirming and praying for those coming to faith*

    v.   *in recognising the decision of faith*

7.5   In an episcopally ordered Church the bishop is the chief minister of the whole process of Christian initiation and is integral to its practice. This finds expression in a number of features of current practice: the requirement of episcopal confirmation (Canon B27; B15A); the canonical requirement that the bishop be given notice of an adult baptism (Canon B24.2); the final say resting with the bishop over a refusal to baptise an infant (Canon B22.2), and over any attempt to bar a baptised person from receiving Communion (Canon B16).

7.6   These duties reflect the particular responsibility of the office of bishop in the process of initiation. This responsibility is not necessarily based on any particular view of the origin or the sacramental character of the episcopal office. It does not require any resolution of the classic controversy as to whether the office of bishop is distinct in its own right or a sort of presidency within the presbyterate.[1] It reflects the particular role of the bishop in the symbolic ordering of an episcopally ordered Church, and needs appropriate expression in the rites of such a Church.

7.7   The bishop is charged with focusing the mission and unity of the Church: as such he has a particular responsibility to keep the way open for enquirers, to oversee their proper formation in the Christian way, and to ensure that they take their rightful place within the wider fellowship of the Church. His ministry in initiation need not be seen as about central-ising control, nor about constraining the welcoming grace of God, nor about being a special channel for the Holy Spirit; its purpose is to enable the process of initiation so that the journey of those coming to faith is protected and affirmed. The focus of initiation is not the needs of the Church nor the bishop; it is about the joyful entry into full Christian life of the person coming to faith.

7.8   This has implications for the ordering of Christian initiation within a diocese. It is integral to the office of bishop to work with and in support of parish clergy and parishes to establish clear, welcoming and strong patterns for the welcome and nurture of new Christians. This not only means that bishops should be seen on occasions as the actual minister of baptism. It also means an active and informed concern with the processes of formation and initiation.

7.9   In recent centuries this aspect of a bishop's work has been focused almost exclusively on their role in confirmation. The effect of this can be to elevate confirmation above baptism and to limit the bishop's opportunity of real contact with those coming to faith.

7.10 In the RCIA the bishop's primary contact with those coming to faith is at the rite called election – the public moment when an individual's decision for Christ is accepted and they enrol for baptism. Confirmation is delegated by the bishop to a presbyter who will preside at the actual baptism unless he himself is to be present.

7.11 In some parts of the catechumenate movement there is a move to involve the bishop not only at the rite of 'election' but also in a more informal way in the period between enrolment for baptism and the baptism itself. It is common for those involved to go on a retreat during this period. The presence of the bishop gives him an opportunity to meet the candidates, hear their stories, and exercise his personal ministry of teaching and encouragment. This may be a practical way for bishops in the Church of England to deepen their pastoral contact with those coming to faith.

Where the more extended process of baptism is adopted as the agreed pattern within a parish, it would be possible to identify points other than confirmation at which a bishop might exercise his ministry in the process of initiation. In such cases it might be possible to follow the Roman Catholic practice of allowing presbyteral confirmation provided that the bishop was personally involved in at least *one* of the following ways:

– presiding at the rite of call and decision in which a candidate was accepted for baptism, confirmation or reaffirmation.

– involvement with the group during the extended period before baptism or related rite.

– presiding at a rite of welcome into episcopal communion in the period after a baptism or related rite.

7.13 There may also be non-liturgical ways in which fellowship with diocese and commitment to the diocese in its mission could be focused. One possibility that is used in other Anglican provinces might be a diocesan badge.

7.14 A further question is whether it would always be necessary for a bishop to preside at the proposed rite to mark the transition to adulthood of young people who have grown up in the Church. There are likely to be good reasons why such a celebration should take place within the life of a local congregation and not necessarily associated with the baptism, confirmation, reaffirmation or reception of other candidates. Under some circumstances this may put an intolerable strain on episcopal diaries and could perhaps on occasions be delegated by the bishop.

Further Implications

One of the categories of people who may be admitted to communion in the Church of England according to Canon B15A (See Appendix 5) is 'any other baptised persons authorised to be admitted under regulations of the General Synod'. This provision has not yet been used but may be the appropriate channel for two groups of people for whom the Church of England has already begun to act:

a. baptised members of other Churches being received into the Church of England according to the rite of reception asked for by the General Synod in its motion of July 1991.

b. those confirmed by presbyters in episcopally ordered Churches in communion with the Church of England – suggested by the Bishop of Grimsby as a follow-up to the approval of the Porvoo Declaration. (See Appendix 4.)

If such a regulation were to be considered it would raise two other issues : the admission of children to communion before confirmation and the position of persons whose confirmation had been delegated by a bishop to a presbyter as part of an extended rite of baptism.

Note

1.   cf. Paul Bradshaw, *The Anglican Ordinal* (Alcuin/SPCK, 1971), pp.31-34, 91-93; R. Hooker, *Ecclesiastical Polity Book* VII.5; *Jerome*, J.N.D. Kelly (Duckworth), pp.147, 212.

Chapter 8

PASTORAL IMPLICATIONS

> *The welcome and nurture of new Christians is one of the most important tasks that faces the Christian community.*

8.1   The Group hopes that the principles set out in this Report may provide a basis for the Church of England in its local, diocesan and national life to review its approaches to initiation, build on good practice, and move towards a greater coherence of approach. Christian initiation is a continuing part of the life of the Church and it would not be desirable or practical to expect every part of the Church to be moving at the same pace. Because of the importance of ecumenical co-operation there might be clear gains in sponsoring various forms of national consultation on Christian initiation; the timing of such consultations will need to take account of the need for adequate experience of developing patterns at the local level.

8.2   Parishes and congregations need to have a clear and developing grasp of their approach to initiation. This implies the involvement of the PCC and wider Church fellowship and not simply an initiative by the clergy. Furthermore such parish policies and approaches must have regard for those particular concerns which are embodied in the bishop's oversight of initiation. This means that each parish would need to identify and own its approach for the welcome and formation of new believers, and these approaches should be worked out in appropriate dialogue with the bishop and should cover :

  – the welcome, formation and sacramental initiation of adult enquirers.

  – an appropriate pattern for responding to requests by non-churchgoing parents for their children's baptism.

  – the appropriate time for admission to communion of children baptised in infancy. Here the first step should be identifying which of the three patterns current in the Church of England is being followed. This would then be taken as the starting point for further planning.

– provision (where appropriate) marking the entry into adulthood of young people growing up within the Church.

8.3   In establishing a welcoming and effective pastoral strategy in each of these four areas a parish needs to have an eye to the sort of considerations set out in this Report and to welcome the concern and interest of the bishop.

Implications for Parishes

8.4   The following are amongst the areas or questions which it may be helpful for a congregation to address as it seeks to establish and implement pastoral strategies for initiation and formation :

The principle of service. Love of neighbour is integral to Christian discipleship. Its manifestation in the life of a congregation creates the context out of which enquiry about discipleship may come. It is also necessary if those coming to faith are to learn the Christian way from the practice of the Church.

Finding natural starting points Any pastoral strategy needs to be rooted in specific pastoral contexts so that it can be seen as a desirable process for particular people. This means reflecting on the existing and natural points of contact with those on the margins of the Church or accessible to it. It also means recognising that any plan is a development or extension of what has already been going on in the life of the Church. It should be seen not as a denial of the past but as an enrichment of current commitments. Another aspect of this involves careful reflection on the culture or cultures of the area in which the Church is set and their implications for the process of welcome and formation.

The importance of welcome. This points not only to the way in which a congregation treats newcomers and visitors, it is also a fundamental principle, embodying the grace and love of God, which needs to infuse any approach to initiation and formation.

The involvement of lay Christians. This is fundamental to any adequate approach to Christian nurture of infants or adults. Clergy cannot give the time and personal attention that proper involvement which Christian formation requires. Lay people are in a position to stand alongside those coming to faith, to sympathise with them, and to journey with them. They also give tangible form to the principle that initiation and formation are the tasks of the whole Church. Lay people should also play

111

a part in the rites that mark and affirm the journey of faith. Co-operative team work is essential. At different stages of the process different abilities and skills will be called upon.

Careful thought has to be given to who chooses people for the different roles and on what basis they are chosen. The leadership of such a group is a powerful position which may attract those who are best not involved. Equally those who would have much to give may be very diffident about what they have to offer. Those who have recently been initiated often have a valued contribution to make. The demands on group leaders may mean that they need to be given the opportunity to review their role; they should not be taken for granted.

The support and training of those involved in these ministries needs to be given careful attention. This will involve time and resources. Deanery, diocesan and ecumenical courses may need to be held. People often want help not so much in how to communicate information as how a group can be run so as to lead people closer to God. Method is as important as content.

Three particular areas of lay involvement are commonly identified:

Sponsor: The sponsor is a companion and friend in the journey of faith. Their function is personal availability and prayer. In some parishes a housebound or elderly church member is also asked to act as a 'prayer sponsor' for an enquirer.

Group leader: This is often a shared task of helping a group of people explore the faith. It involves skills in handling a group as well as some knowledge of the content of Christian belief. Group leaders may previously have been sponsors within the process.

Co-ordinator: Variously titled, this refers to the task of overseeing and resourcing the process of formation and the life of the groups. This post might initially be a role for the clergy but need not necessarily be so. The clergy's primary task is to see that tasks are carefully allocated and that people are given appropriate initial training and ongoing support.

The necessity of ownership by the congregation. Care and time needs to be taken to help a church understand that the welcome and nurture of new Christians is the responsibility of the whole people of God. This will involve careful presentation and planning. In many situations it will require a progressive process involving clergy, churchwardens, lay ministers such as readers, and the PCC, before seeking to gain the willing consent and involvement of the whole church. It is particularly important to give the PCC time to understand the underlying vision, contribute to the process of establishing a pastoral strategy, estimate the cost and own the resulting approach. Time must be taken in allowing the emergence of a clear common purpose which carries the genuine consent of all concerned. It may well be appropriate for the bishop to play a part in helping a church explore the nature and priority of initiation and formation.

The congregation need to have an active continuing involvement with any pastoral strategy particularly in building bridges within the community, in welcoming visitors and enquirers, in identifying sponsors and leaders, as well as in public and private prayer. There is something to be said for having a special time of year (e.g. early summer) when the whole church concentrates in prayer and action on bringing in new enquirers.

The process of adopting a pastoral strategy for initiation may raise fundamental questions about the priorities of the congregation. Many churches are organised around the needs and wishes of insiders. This can be true at the level of formal (PCC, parish organisations) and informal (leadership teams, house groups) structures. The attempt to function at both levels can lead to certain churches melting down into activism while leaving little room for effective outreach. Gearing a church towards the support and welcome of those on and beyond the edge of its life can result in a substantial reorientation of a congregation's life. This may, in turn, lead to significant simplification of its life. One commentator writes,

> The basic question is, 'What are sufficient iron rations for a Christian?'. The answer may well be regular reception of the eucharist ... private prayer ... an accepting group. All else is luxury. The Church should provide these but little else – except appropriate support to people in their work/home environment and helping others to find faith.

Investigating co-operation. Serious consideration should be given to work with neighbouring churches, Anglican or other, in evolving and working a pastoral strategy for initiation. This could be the churches of a town, area, deanery or neighbourhood. In certain contexts a number of churches working together might find it easier to sustain the demands of supporting the process of initiation. In such cases it would be particularly important to have a clear common understanding of the pastoral strategy being adopted. Where there is no co-operation, unhealthy competition can develop or people on the edge of church life may get little sense of what Christian initiation involves.

Human-sized groups. The easiest place to share faith is in one-to-one encounter or in a small group. The best sized group is one where there is time and space for everyone to be able to contribute but in which anyone wanting to keep quiet can do so – probably eight to twelve people. This allows for close (but not claustrophobic) relationships, and for confidence and trust to be built up. The group needs to be small enough to fit into the rooms available, to be able to eat together (as derivation of the word companion – with bread – suggests), to be able to go and do things together as a group. It needs to be large enough to avoid people feeling embarrassed or conspicuous especially in times of prayer and worship.

It is important that the exploration of the faith stays close to daily life as perceived by people in the group or familiar to them. Essentially it must be their questions which are asked. The startling ignorance of quite basic Christian teaching shown by many people (even natural leaders within a congregation) reflects their being given information when they were not interested in it, and so not able or ready to receive it. People want time to ask questions, exchange ideas and even argue, the right to personal conviction, and space to be provisional and unsure; this needs to be allowed for and respected.

Thought and care needs to be given to the life and development of the group and particularly to the overarching aim of integrating new Christians into the life and service of the congregation. Oversight of the group includes helping to identify what the group needs and making appropriate resources available to them. The closing of a group at the completion of its task can require particular care and may need to be marked by appropriate celebration.

Consideration must be given as to whether sponsors should always or sometimes attend group sessions or simply be available to individuals outside the group meetings. Points at issue are the time required, the size and frequency of groups, the temperament and style of the group leaders, the possible contribution of sponsors in modelling commitment, and the way in which the groups work. A possible disadvantage of sponsors being present is that their numbers can overwhelm or unbalance the group. On the other hand it may help their support of their candidate and lead to the deepening of their own faith.

The principle of integration One of the important lessons from the catechumenate is its emphasis on integration. This affects both the process of formation and the goal of initiation:

THE WAY.   *Discipleship means learning*
                to worship with the church
                to grow in prayer
                to listen to the scriptures
                to serve our neighbour

GOAL.   *The goal of initiation is*
                relationship with God the Holy Trinity
                life and worship with the church
                service and witness in the world

One of the purposes of the use of liturgical rites in marking the journey to faith is to deepen the bonds between congregation and those finding their way in Christ.

This theme of integration also means that careful thought needs to be given to the way the developing life of an enquirers' group is related to the liturgical life of the parish. Parishes which give a high profile to the Church's year are likely find a natural focus for initiation in one of the festivals of the Church. Others will also need to give careful attention to this aspect of integration.

The importance of rite. Prayer is an integral part of the journey in faith. Care needs to be given to adapting and using appropriate liturgical rites to mark both the developing life of an enquirers' group and also the support of enquirers and others in public worship.

Respect for human process. The image of the Way expresses the developing character of the journey into faith. The starting point and natural pace of the individuals involved needs to be respected within any parish programme or strategy. People's formation should not be squeezed into the demands of the annual parochial timetable. It is integral to the notion of enquirer as adopted in this Report that this position should be available to people with little Christian knowledge and background who may need a deep grounding in the Christian Way.

A similar open-endess needs to characterise the development of structures and strategies within a parish. Although clarity about goals is desirable at the start, the programme itself will have to be built up gradually, with each part developed in the light of those exploring the faith as well as local needs, customs and resources. Taking initiation seriously will change the perspective of clergy and congregation. Pastoral strategies will themselves need to be seen not as once for all policy decisions but implying development and review.

Expecting the presence of God. Christian initiation is not about socialising people into the rules and practice of a club. It involves encounter with the dynamic presence and mission of the living God. This involves an expectation of God's presence and an openness and discernment towards new developments. Enquirers need to be encouraged to discover the presence of God in their lives and to discern and embrace their vocation in the world. The Church needs to be willing to learn from those on a journey into faith, to expect new gifts from the Holy Spirit, and to pray for the developing ministry of all involved in its life. A parochial strategy for initiation will involve the Church itself in a journey of faith.

Implications for the Bishop's Ministry

8.5 The purpose and character of the bishop's ministry in Christian initiation is discussed more fully in chapter 7 (paras 7.4-7.14). It arises from his responsibility for focusing the mission and unity of the Church. Its aim is to ensure the joyful entry into full Christian life of the person coming to faith. He incarnates the reality of joining and belonging to a wider community than the congregation. His ministry is to empower the process and himself be committed to it. The bishop exercises his ministry in initiation in partnership with his fellow bishops in the diocese and with others whom he may choose to involve. It is of the essence of this ministry that it is embodied and facilitative; while there needs to be realism about the demands on individuals, this aspect of initiation has to focus on contact between persons;

1. The commitment of the bishop to initiation does not imply either omnipresence or tight control. As with all others involved in initiation,

it needs to be characterised by humility towards the newcomer and an openness to the presence of God.

2. The bishop's ministry is personal and not simply structural or symbolic. The bishop has a role in helping parishes identify and develop appropriate patterns and schemes for initiation.

3. It is part of the bishop's role in initiation to ensure that all those on a journey to faith confidently take their place within the wider fellowship of the Church of England.

4. One way in which the bishop's oversight may be expressed could be by encouraging a parish to link up with a diocesan network of parishes adopting a similar pastoral strategy. This may be particularly appropriate as a way of linking parishes exploring a catechumenal approach to the initiation of adults and young people.

5. The bishop, through whatever people or structures are thought most suitable, must be in close touch with the parish, offering whatever support, materials, encouragement, etc. are appropriate.

6. The bishop will need to face in himself what he is prepared to offer. He will obviously need to identify what role he is prepared to fill in the ritual process. But he will also want to exercise his teaching ministry in the educational process. How this latter may be done will depend on his own gifts and talents. Bishops may well wish to be available to parishes, groups of parishes, deaneries, etc. A bishop might offer a teaching module to parishes that could be used at an appropriate stage in the parish scheme of initiation.

7. The diocese will need to monitor initiation and formation within the diocese so that it can own the process and advise the bishop.

8. The bishop will need to acknowledge the demands that these schemes will make on diocesan structures. The equivalent of the General Synod Board of Education's Voluntary Continuing Educational Committee may be a paradigm, with its role of bringing together work with children, young people and adults.

9. The Church will need to provide suitable CME for bishops to help them exercise their teaching ministry more effectively.

10. There will be a need to identify resources available to parishes to assist them in their responsibilities.

Resources

8.6   Parishes should not feel alone as they respond to their baptismal calling and to their vital role in the welcome and nurture of new Christians. There are many sources of resource or wisdom on which they can call. These include: voluntary societies; Christian publishers; diocesan officers, boards and resource centres; regional theological institutions; sector ministers with relevant skills; and ecumenical agencies and personnel. There will often be valuable experience or knowledge in nearby parishes or other churches. Networks of parishes facing similar problems or adopting similar approaches can often provide a way forward. Bishops need to be seen as a resource and need to play a part in identifying resources and fostering good practice. As churches seek to rise to their responsiblities for initiation and formation, there is likely to be a need for regional and national centres, possibly on an ecumenical basis, to make available resources and appropriate training.

8.7   The keywords of partnership and coherence point towards a style of working which could help individual churches that are struggling to find a viable approach to Christian initiation or to face a daunting set of practical problems in implementing their vision. Such co-operation could help rescue the practice of Christian initiation from its present fragmentation and lead to a clearer witness to the new creation in Christ which baptism itself proclaims.

Into the Future

8.8   At the heart of Christian initiation is the picture of the life of faith as a journey. It is a powerful picture both in common human experience and in the great sweep of the story of God's people. When the Church begins to take seriously the calling and identity implied in baptism it finds itself committed to a process that it cannot completely control and whose outcome it cannot know. The main theme of Stephen's speech in Acts 7 can be expressed simply: God does not repeat himself; the people of God need to respond to the mission of the Holy Spirit. Both Acts and John's Gospel portray the Holy Spirit, not only as enabling the Church's witness to Christ, but also as active beyond the Church creating faith in Christ and bringing into existence the new humanity.

8.9   To travel with the Spirit does not mean forgetting the story of the past nor neglecting the food and guidance that God provides for the journey. Taking the welcome of newcomers seriously will deepen the Church's understanding of the scriptures, of baptism, and of eucharist, as well as of its own history. Nor does travelling with the Spirit imply incoherence and fragmentation; it will require discipline and coherence in establishing new believers in the Christian Way. But responding to Christ's mission will involve surprise and change as the Church meets God's Spirit in those coming to faith. The Church needs to look for and expect the presence of the Holy Spirit if it is to hear God's voice on the way. Policies and strategies are important; they need to be seen against the mission and work of God they seek to serve.

Appendix 1

FROM THE GENERAL SYNOD DEBATE JULY 1991

Motion passed by General Synod on 13th July 1991
The motion was put and carried in the following amended form:

That this Synod

a. affirm the traditional sequence of Baptism Confirmation – admission to Communion as normative in the Church of England;

b. accept that within this sequence Confirmation can take place at an early age when this is deemed appropriate by the parish priest and the bishop;

c. ask the Liturgical Commission to prepare a series of rites described as Route Three in GS Misc 366 for the renewal of baptismal vows, for the reception of members of another church, and for reconciliation and healing;

d. ask the Liturgical Commission to prepare a rite of Adult Commitment as stated in paragraph 134 of GS Misc 365;

e. ask the House of Bishops in consultation with the Board of Education, Board of Mission and the Liturgical Commission to prepare a paper on patterns of nurture in the faith, including the Catechumenate.

The General Synod accepted an amendment to delete one section of the original motion as proposed by the House of Bishops. The section deleted was as follows :

agree that experiments of admission to Communion before Confirmation should be discontinued at a rate which gives due regard to the pastoral difficulties in individual dioceses and parishes.

Appendix 2

EXTRACT FROM THE FINDINGS OF THE INTERNATIONAL
ANGLICAN LITURGICAL CONSULTATION, TORONTO, 1991

Recommendations on Principles of Christian Initiation

a.   The renewal of baptismal practice is an integral part of mission and evangelism. Liturgical texts must point beyond the life of the church to God's mission in the world.

b.   Baptism is for people of all ages, both adults and infants. Baptism is administered after preparation and instruction of the candidates, or where they are unable to answer for themselves, of their parent(s) or guardian(s).

c.   Baptism is complete sacramental initiation and leads to participation in the eucharist. Confirmation and other rites of affirmation have a continuing pastoral role in the renewal of faith among the baptized but are in no way to be seen as a completion of baptism or as necessary for admission to communion.

d.   The catechumenate is a model for preparation and formation for baptism. We recognize that its constituent liturgical rites may vary in different cultural contexts.

e.   Whatever language is used in the rest of the baptismal rite, both the profession of faith and the baptismal formula should continue to name God as Father, Son, and Holy Spirit.

f.   Baptism once received is unrepeatable and any rites of renewal must avoid being misconstrued as rebaptism.

g.   The pastoral rite of confirmation may be delegated by the bishop to a presbyter.

Section 2 of the Toronto Statement

BAPTISM, MISSION, AND MINISTRY

God's Mission

1.   Mission is first and foremost God's mission to God's world. 'As the Father has sent me, even so I send you' (John 20.21). This mission is made visible in the person and work of Jesus and is entrusted by him to the church.

2.   'When the Advocate comes, whom I will send to you from the Father, the Spirit of truth, who comes from the Father, he will testify on my behalf' (John 15.26). The primary agent of mission is God the Holy Spirit, who brings into existence a community of faith to embody this mission and to make God's new order manifest in a broken world. 'You will receive power when the Holy Spirit has come upon you; and you will be my witnesses' (Acts 1.8; cf. John 15.27). The church needs the empowering of the Spirit to play its part in God's mission; it is called to proclaim the gospel, nurture people in the faith, care for the needy, and seek to transform the unjust structures of society.[1]

3.   All that the church does is expressive of this mission, when it is true to its nature. This must be so of its worship. As the church remembers its calling and waits on God in prayer, it is empowered for mission. Baptism in particular declares the gospel of God's saving love in Christ, establishes the church as Christ's body, and marks the individual believers as those called to participate in the work of the kingdom.

Baptism and evangelism

4.   We welcome the developing awareness of the dignity and significance of baptism in the church, and believe that this needs to be consolidated by emphasising the integral relation of evangelism and baptism. The journey into faith involves a process that includes awareness of God, recognition of God's work in Christ, entering into the Christian story through the scriptures, turning to Christ as Lord, incorporation into the body of Christ, nurture within the worshipping community, and being equipped and commissioned for ministry and mission within God's world. An adequate practice

122

of baptism will recognize all these dimensions and will enable the church to play its full part in accomp-anying people on this journey. We therefore welcome the rediscovery of a pastoral and liturgical pattern which marks and celebrates these stages.

Come and see: a bridge to the life of faith

5.   Evangelism in our Communion often involves groups for enquirers and new believers which also include mature believers who accompany and nurture them. Many provinces recognize the status of catechumen in the preparation for baptism, have a rite for the admission to the catechumenate, and have rich community-based patterns of Christian formation. Patterns of formation vary greatly, taking different forms in isolated rural communities, societies where natural community is important, and atomized urban society. The strength and vitality of a culture's commitment to Christianity also affects patterns of personal formation. We recognize a debt to the Roman Catholic Church in making liturgical provision for marking the catechumen's journey into faith, through the Rite of Christian Initiation of Adults (RCIA). We welcome also the initiative in the Episcopal Church (USA) in making available in its Book of Occasional Services (second edition, 1988) rites for the catechumenate for the unbaptized and similar rites for baptized persons who seek a renewal of faith.

6.   The catechumenal process begins with the welcome of individuals, the valuing of their story, the recognition of the work of God in their lives, the provision of sponsors to accompany their journey, and the engagement of the whole Christian community in both supporting them and learning from them. It seeks to promote personal formation of the new believer in four areas: formation in the Christian tradition as made available in the scriptures, development in personal prayer, incorporation in the worship of the church, and ministry in society, particularly to the powerless, the sick, and all in need. The catechumenal process commonly includes four distinct stages, with the transition between them liturgically marked within the assembly:

– enquiry,
– formation, properly called the catechumenate,

– immediate preparation, sometimes know as candidacy,

– post-baptismal reflection, or mystagogy.

7. We see this revival of the catechumenate as strengthening the ministry and mission of the church in a number of ways: it offers those seeking faith a way of exploring Christian discipleship and taking their place in the life and mission of the church; it respects the integrity and humanity of those seeking faith and avoids the danger of squeezing them into a pre-arranged and scheduled program; it challenges all the baptized to take evangelism seriously, and to become more effective in it. The catechumenate provides a model for other processes of personal formation. It restores to the community of faith its essential role as the minister of baptism. It challenges the church through the questioning and enthusiasm of new believers. It subverts the dominance of the clergy by recognizing the responsibility and ministry of all the baptized.

The Baptizing Community

8. 'One Lord, one faith, one baptism' (Eph. 4.5). We see the catechumenal process affirming and celebrating the baptismal identity of the whole community. As people participate in the process, whether as enquirers, catechumens, candidates, and initiates, or as sponsors, catechists, and clergy, the one baptism by which all are incorporated in the one body of Christ will be apprehended. In this way the whole church is formed as a participatory community, one whose members share life with one another, while at the same time being conjoined to the missionary purpose of God for which baptism calls the community into existence. Through the lens of baptism the people of God begin to see that lay ministry is important not simply because it allows an interested few to exercise their individual ministries, but because the ministry and mission of God in the church is the responsibility of all the baptized community.

Baptism: fount of justice and ministry

9. 'For as the body is one and has many members, and all the members of the body, though many, are one body, so it is with Christ. For in the one Spirit we were all baptized into one body – Jews or Greeks, slaves or free – and we were all made to drink of one Spirit' (1 Cor. 12.12-13). Baptism affirms the royal dignity of every

Christian and their call and empowering for active ministry within the mission of the church. The renewal of baptismal practice, with a consequent awareness of the standing of the baptized in the sight of God, therefore has an important part to play in renewing the church's respect for all the people of God. A true understanding of baptism will bring with it a new expectancy about the ministry of each Christian. It will also provide an important foundation for allowing different Christians their true and just place within the life of the church. This is of particular significance for categories of Christians who are marginalized by church or society. Baptism gives Christians a vision of God's just order; it makes the church a sign and instrument of the new world that God is establishing; it empowers Christians to strive for justice and peace within society.

The Gospel for the Baptized

10. 'Do you not know that all of us who have been baptized into Christ Jesus were baptized into his death?' (Rom. 6.3). There are many reasons why the gospel should be preached to those who have been baptized. They may have fallen away from Christian fellowship and discipleship. They may never have had the will or the opportunity to respond to God's gracious gift offered to them in baptism. They may have continued within the life of the church without a deep personal grasp of the reality signified in baptism. It is important for the integrity of the church's sacramental practice that such people are not treated as if they have not been baptized. For this reason the baptized are not to be called catechumens. An opportunity for them to renew their baptismal commitment may be provided through a rite of confirmation or reaffirmation of faith; such a rite should reinforce rather than undermine their awareness of baptism. In many situations it may be helpful to provide personal formation similar to the catechumenate, including the involvement of sponsors as companions on the way. The Episcopal Church (U.S.A.) has made a valuable contribution in creating a series of rites to mark such a journey of renewal. As in the ancient practice of the order of penitents, Ash Wednesday and Maundy Thursday frame the final stage of reaffirmation. In other cultures and contexts other appropriate forms could be created to support people in their return to the dignity and ministry of baptism.

Parents and sponsors

11.   When infants are to be baptized, parents and sponsors are the main focus of preparation and formation, since parents have an important part to play in the spiritual formation of children. In the past, parents and sponsors have undergone meagre (or no) preparation. Christian formation and the renewal of the baptismal process demand that this change. A few classes which simply instruct in a small amount of theology do not provide the necessary renewal of faith. What is required is a holistic approach in which the goal is formation, not simply the provision of information. The catechumenal model for the renewal of faith is helpful for this. A programme on catechumenal lines, with the involvement of lay persons, will help build bridges between the local community and parents and sponsors as well as encourage and help them to renew their own faith commitment. (See, for example, the *Book of Occasional Services*, second edition 1988).

The catechumenate for infants or children?

12.   The formation of a catechumenate for young children has been discussed in a number of places. It might be useful to admit to the catechumenate those young children whose parents/sponsors are going through a renewal process as described above. Until the parents are ready to accept the faith responsibilities in presenting their children for baptism, the children may continue as catechumens. It might also be useful to admit to the catechumenate those children whose parents choose to delay their baptism (for whatever reason). Proposals for adapting and using some of the liturgical rites of the catechumenate merit further investigation and experimentation. Limited experience has shown some initial benefit in doing this. A warning, however, should be sounded in this discussion: some clergy and parishes may be tempted to use the admission of young children to the catechumenate as a roundabout and non-confrontational way of refusing baptism. Therefore, infants should not be admitted as catechumens without an expectation of continuing nurture and formation. The whole area of a catechumenate for children needs to be explored further.

13. It may be helpful to identify three areas of possible confusion or difficulty :

14.1 Terminology : The word 'catechumenate' is often used as a shorthand term for the whole journey of faith leading to baptism and the emerging ministry of the baptized. In contemporary rites, 'catechumenate' describes only one of four periods in the journey into faith.

14.2 The term is often used as a synonym for a similar process provided for those already baptized. We would urge that the term 'catechumen' and catechumenate' should only be used for the unbaptized, while the term 'catechumenal process' may be used for any pattern of Christian formation.

14.3 The term 'catechumen' is regarded by some as antiquarian. However, there are advantages to using a word that resonates with the historic practice of the church. At the same time, simple terms may need to be found for liturgical rites that mark the stages of the journey in faith. 'Baptism', 'baptismal process', and 'reaffirmation of baptism' may be better general terms than 'catechumenate'. 'Initiation' also has wide currency although it may give rise to difficulties in cultures with developed rituals to mark birth or puberty.

15. Some believe that the catechumenal approach to baptism is in conflict with the New Testament practice of baptism on profession of faith. They think it may undermine the priority of grace made explicit by placing baptism firmly at the start of a person's public discipleship. Three points diminish this difficulty :

15.1 The period between welcoming enquirers as catechumens and the acknowledgement of their call as candidates for baptism must not be seen as a period of probation to see whether their discipleship matches up to certain criteria. All practices that appear to apply this sort of probation must be carefully avoided. This period should rather be seen as a period of growth and discernment in which both individual and church are involved.

15.2 The practice of baptism in the New Testament cannot be separated from the process of entry into the gospel,[2] nor from the Christian community's welcome and reception of the candidate.

Baptism was not simply a formal, official act devoid of profound personal encounter and communication. If baptism is properly to effect what it represents, the church as well as the candidate must be fully and meaningfully present for the sacramental act. In most social contents this will imply something like the sort of extended process to be found in the ancient and modern phased rites of initiation. 'Catechumenate' and 'candidacy' should not be seen as stages of preparation for an eventual baptism, but as part of the extended process of baptism: conversion and baptism unfolding together.

15.3   It may be helpful to make a clear distinction between the stages of 'enquirer' and 'catechumen' on the one hand, in which the decision for Christ and baptism is being made, and the stages of 'candidate' and 'neophyte', in which candidate and church are involved together in an extended and full celebration of the baptismal reality.

16.   Another concern raised by the catechumenal approach to baptism is a fear that it will raise barriers between the church and the surrounding culture. Some are anxious not to alienate those who are associated with the church as God-fearers. Where the church is a culturally distinct community in the context of a plurality of religious faiths, some are concerned that baptism may wrongly be seen as involving the denial of one's cultural heritage. Properly practised, the catechumenal approach to baptism can lower the barriers between church and society in two ways: first, it creates a bridge to enable people outside the Church to find their way in; second, it encourages the church to value and respect the cultural heritage of those coming to faith.

Notes

1.   *Bonds of Affection*, Proceedings of ACC-6 (Anglican Consultative Council, London, 1985), pp.48f

2.   [It may be that 'church' should be read here in place of 'gospel'.]

Appendix 3

CONTEMPORARY CATECHUMENATE PRACTICE IN THE CHURCH OF ENGLAND

by David Sanderson   (Church Army)

[This account is based on a survey of 30 churches involved in the catechumenate in 1992-1993. The term 'enquirer' is used of what the RCIA call the pre-catechumenate stage.]

Who are Joining Catechumenate Groups?

The Catechumenate in the early Church was used to lead enquirers to baptism and Christian maturity. However, current practice is not so clear cut. In fact, we are attracting three distinct categories of people:

i)   Those for whom the process was originally intended – i.e. potential new Christians desiring instruction and baptism.

ii)   Those baptised who desire confirmation; such a category can be quite mixed. It includes those from other traditions, perhaps lapsed, wishing to become Anglicans; those brought up in the church seeking confirmation; and those, baptised as infants, whose link with the Church has been broken and are now seeking a vital faith. The majority of modern 'catechumens' are in this category.

iii)   Regular church members who want a 'refresher course'. Such people sometimes become sponsors.

Such a diversity can produce problems. One church started the course with 13 people, eight of whom were regular church attenders and five who were unfamiliar with the church. Such a combination created problems as the group faced up to its agenda. Those unfamiliar with Christian teaching had questions about the issues of daily life, while the others were more interested in 'churchy' things. The problem was resolved by splitting into two groups to enable them to pursue their own separate agendas. Also, as the catechumenal rites are designed for the journey to faith, most churches had nothing to offer those who came on a refresher course, but a few did find ways of including them. The Episcopal Church in USA has faced this problem and provides rites to enable the baptised to reaffirm their baptismal covenant.[1]

The Catechumenate and the Christian Year

A common timetable for the catechumenate is September to Pentecost and includes baptism at Easter. In this way all the main liturgical celebrations of the faith are linked with the church year. In the Church of England catechumenate programmes are determined by confirmation dates. Therefore, some, for example, have run from January to September. Thus missing out on Advent and Christmas. While churches have achieved successful catechumenate programmes without the traditional timetable, it seems a pity not to take full advantage of the church year. If the catechumenate is to be taken seriously then some strategic planning to enable bishops to be available within the octave of Easter for confirmations is required. A pilot catechumenal project[2] in Sheffield Diocese which involved about 14 churches included a joint confirmation service at the Cathedral on Easter Eve. Clearly, this was one practical answer to the problem.

The Gathering of Potential Disciples

The first stage of the catechumenate process, the pre-catechumenate or enquiry stage, can last from a few months up to a couple years. During this period people who are interested in knowing more about Christian faith are gathered together. How are such people recruited? Various ways have been used, notices at church services, meetings of church organisations and parish or community magazines. One church, albeit using another form of small group evangelism, had some response even from a beetle drive. In fact, any church-related organisation can be used. Key people to invite are those who have been contacted through the occasional offices and friends of church members. Some churches advertised outside church circles with a leaflet for general distribution in a local newspaper. On the whole the more general advertising did not yield a lot, though one Vicar reported that a young man of 25, whom he had met two years previously, joined the group through this general publicity.

As part of this initial gathering together many churches invited people to some kind of social. Attendance at these introductory meetings varied, but some reported as many as 20 people attending who were at best infrequent attenders at church. After the meeting people were invited to attend a series of Christian enquiry meetings. In most cases a small group wanted to take things further. One church reported as many as 11 people who wished to join the enquiry group.

Churches in mining areas and on council estates experienced difficulty in getting the process started. The absence of church/community networks in such areas made the collecting of potential disciples difficult. A few of the churches did not get any response at all. Also, in such areas, even where there was good success one year, some found it difficult to sustain a second year because they had used up their contacts in the first year. Particularly in these areas, though it is true generally, there is a need to give high priority to developing relationships with the community, both formally by the institutional church and informally by church members. Effective evangelism can only take place where a network of relationships exists to support it.

Two churches used the *Good News Down the Street* (GNDS)[3] programme as part of the enquiry stage for the catechumenate and found it a good way of preparing for what was to follow. One of these churches, which visits an area of the parish every year with a view to setting up GDNS groups, reports that in three years almost 70 adults have been baptised and confirmed, and more who having already been baptised have been confirmed. Clearly, this approach is something other churches could consider.

Stages at Which People Drop Out

The very structure of catechumenate asks people to opt into the relevant stages as evidence of their desire to continue on the journey. It also gives people the opportunity to drop out if they so desire. Some people left after the very first enquiry meeting as they realised more fully what was proposed. As one might expect, a crucial decision is whether to move from the enquiry stage to the catechumenate proper. Some who had committed themselves to attending the enquiry meetings did not take the next step. One or two churches found that the third stage, after the end of the catechumenate proper, was a time when people left. However, not all churches marked the stages so sharply, but even in these some people dropped out as the implications of the process became clearer. Churches which made regular Sunday worship obligatory for the catechumenate stage appear to have increased the probability of people not proceeding further. Other churches which made no such demand found that some, at least, realised they could not continue without the experience of regular worship.

Reasons for people withdrawing included that in their own judgement they were not ready to proceed, or just that it was 'not for them'. Family pressure, homework or evening class commitments were also mentioned. The summer break was a factor in one case and others found the discussion element difficult.

Finding a Name

Some find the word 'Catechumenate' is unfortunate or obscure, others disagree and like this ancient ecclesiastical title. Alternatives that have been used include, 'Adult Quest', 'Christian Growth', 'Light Fantastic', 'Journey to Faith' or even 'The New Wine'. In some churches it continues to be known simply as 'The Confirmation Class'!

Analysis of Numbers of People involved in the Process

Sixteen churches provided information about the numbers of people involved. A breakdown into categories, where that information allowed, appears on the next page. Some listed as 'Not linked' were lapsed members of other denominations. The other categories were defined as follows: 'Outer Fringe', attend Church three or four times a year; 'Attend Monthly', attend about once a month; 'Regular Attender', attend three Sundays a month or more.

One church gave information over three years. They had developed a group sponsorship. The numbers provided include the sponsors 28 (2 catechumens), 15 (4 catechumens), 16 (5 catechumens).

That eight churches indicated they had people not linked with the church and seven people from the outer fringe gives cause for hope, but it is not clear whether this level of achievement could be sustained over a longer period. In most instances the numbers are small, so the general trend is that the work is with a few people over an extended period of time.

Teaching and Supporting Roles

The catechumenate is an accompanied journey and the enquirers/catechumens are assisted on the journey by sponsors, catechists or teachers and clergy. How are the roles of such people interpreted?

BEGAN	RELATIONSHIP TO CHURCH						COMPLETED		
	Not linked	Outer Fringe	Attend Monthly	Regular Attender	Not Bapt	Not Con	Total	Bapt	Con
1		Lapsed	Presbyt.				1	1	1
4						2	2		2
5	2	1		2		3	5		3
6		3		3	1	6	6	1	6
7		includes	2	children		7			7
9	3		3	3	2	5	7	2	5
11		2	2	7	1	7	8	1	8
11		2	3	6		5	10		5
12	1	5	4	2	1	8	8	1	4
13	7			6			7	1	3
13	5			6			11		3
14		still in progress			3				
15			15				6		6
17	16			1	2	15	17	2	17
20	7			13 (10 sponsors)			16	5	
21	11	6	4	(5 children)			21	1	21

i)   The functions of *sponsors* included befriending the catechumens, giving prayer support and faith sharing. It was not always easy to find the right sponsors and some churches opted for a group sponsorship, where the potential new Christians were adopted by a group of sponsors without them being paired on a one to one basis. One vicar said of the sponsors that it was they who break the ice for the unchurched and the lapsed. In some churches sponsors and enquirers were introduced to each other at the very beginning of the enquiry process, while others waited until the catechumenate stage.

ii)   Some clergy see themselves as the proper people to teach. Other clergy think teaching the faith is a lay role as well as a clerical one. There was also a third group of clergy who were currently leading the teaching sessions themselves, but were working towards the day when the laity would take on the role.

When approached, the potential lay catechists in one church were taken aback at being asked to share in this task. They had three training sessions and were expected to work together as a team. Clearly, training is required. However, where there are lay catechists, it is generally recognised they do a good job.

In another church the clergy kept a very low profile while lay catechists took the initiative. When the time for the confirmation came the clergy did not think they knew the communicants as well as they should have done. A proper balance is required between the role of the clergy and of the laity.

iii)   The sharp division between the roles of sponsors and catechists is not always evident. A number of churches have combined the roles so that lay people take part both in the teaching and supporting the potential Christians. One church devised a scheme where the full catechumenate group met once a fortnight. The alternate weeks these sponsor/catechists (in this case called 'walkers' because they journeyed alongside the catechumens) met to reflect on the previous week and to prepare for the next. In the full meeting they taught and shared with the catechumens on a one to one basis. A development like this not only enabled the 'walkers' to learn while they are doing, it also provided opportunity for the development of leaders for future catechumenal groups.

iv)   Whatever *the role of the clergy* one thing is clear. Someone needs to have pastoral oversight of the catechumens. People coming into the church with very little Christian background will need a lot of help. Some will need practical help such as finding their way around the Bible or prayer book. For others there will be moral issues to come to terms with. Support will be required as they begin to find their way into a new Christian life.

A large multi-church parish with a number of years of catechumenal experience has worked out and documented the clergy role. The document includes the following statements. 'The catechumenate points up the role and responsibility of the whole Church in nurturing newcomers... Clergy will be part of the catechumenate team in varying degrees without necessarily having responsibility for running the catechumenate. Catechists represent the congregation in their role and ministry.' One of the clergy acts as a chaplain to the catechumenate groups and the chaplain's specific tasks include being involved directly with the catechumenate team in planning and continuing developments as well as in providing pastoral care for them. The chaplain presides at some of the rites and gets to know the enquirers/catechumens personally. Individual Team Vicars also have a responsibility for the cate-chumens in their own congregation. It is recognised that they are best placed to identify potential catechumens, to get to know those from their own congregation, discern their readiness to go forward to the next step and also to preside at some of the rites. They are also resource people for the catech-umenate team and sometimes present topics at the catechu-menate groups.[4]

The Liturgical Rites

The rites mark the various stages of the journey. The main rites are Entry to Catechumenate proper, Enrolment (or Election) which provides the entry into the second stage and Confirmation or Baptism. There are other rites most of which are performed in Lent. The main rites, ideally, take place in church at the Eucharist; some of the others can take place in more private settings. The idea of up-front rites in church for people who are in the process of becoming church members seems somewhat frightening – so much so that one church omitted all the rites, with the exception of Confirmation. However, most churches think the rites are important and attempt to overcome this problem. Some rehearse the rites in private first. With the very first rite, the entry to the catechumenate, one church met the new catechumens at the church door where they welcomed them and prayed with them before they led them to their seats, thus avoiding the up front appearance. Sponsors have a distinct contribution to make during the rites. They stand alongside the catechumens during the ceremony and provide moral support.

In general it was thought that once the catechumens had become used to the idea of the rites they valued them. The rites appear to be valued for at least the following reasons:

a) The congregation are included in the ministry to new members.
b) The potential new members are brought to the notice of the congregation.
c) The rites mark the progress of the new member.
d) The symbolism in the rites is part of the growth process.
e) The catechumens are affirmed and accepted by the church.

A variety of forms of the rites were used. Some churches wrote their own. Among Catholic churches there was a tendency to use a modified version of the RCIA.

Teaching Programmes

A key element in any catechumenal programme is sharing together. It is recognised that the catechumens will have much to contribute as well as having questions they need to have answered. There must therefore be space for open sharing, discussion and reflection. Some practitioners are prepared to a large extent to let the catechumens set the agenda, though others are more directive. These two approaches are not mutually exclusive. To do justice to both, yet other practitioners have a check list which enables them to form an agenda on the basis of issues raised by the potential catechumen, but at the same time to add any elements deemed to be essential that have been omitted.

A variety of teaching material is used, and many preferred to produce their own home grown material arguing that because no two groups are the same, they need different material each time. Preparatory material which was thought to be of value included *Christian Basics* (CPAS), *Christian Basics: An outline of the Faith* (Company of Mission Priests), *Follow Me* (Additional Curates Society), *Good News Down the Street*, M. Wooderson (Grove), *Proclamation and Offering: Story and Choice*, A.W.Schwab and W.A.Yon (Office of Evangelization Ministries USA), and *Step by Step*, M.T.Molar (Brown ROA, Dubuque, Iowa).

What Follows the Catechumenal Programme?

Some churches saw the importance of keeping the groups together after the formal process had concluded by setting up further groups for Bible study and fellowship. Such a move would appear to be important as there is evidence of people dropping out after the formal process is over. Perhaps this is almost to be expected if folk suddenly lose the benefits of being a member of a small group. Yet with some clergy there was a reluctance to set up such groups. However, research with other forms of small group evangelism indicates that a high percentage of people continue if they are integrated into further small groups when each phase comes to an end. Catechumenate practitioners could learn from this insight.

Evidence of Spiritual Change, Growth and Renewal

Churches reported a number of good things which had happened as part of the catechumenal process. A man of 30 who had been something of a 'wide boy' discovered real meaning to life and spoke to his friends on the bus to work about his new faith. They could not believe it! His wife who thought she had faith, felt left behind and is seeking to recapture the faith she had as a teenager. A teenage girl who was very much on the periphery of the church is now active in the Sunday school and in the singing group. Others reported that people recognised that God was with them and the other members of the group. Long-term members of churches, acting as sponsors, found new life through faith sharing. Some joined social action groups and others became more involved in the church. Attitudes to moral issues changed.

One vicar commented on the difference it had made to the church as a whole: 'We are now on the look out for people to join the next group – inherently evangelistic.' Another church, rightly, saw that catechumenate was not simply a better way of training confirmees, it was, in itself, a total mission strategy. They restructured to facilitate the inclusion of the new insights they had discovered.

Limitations to the Catechumenate

While there are some excellent benefits to be gained from the catechumenal process, it does have limitations. Not everybody, for example, is comfortable in a small group. For such people it may prove a stumbling block. Other routes for helping people to baptism and confirmation will need to be available. Further, churches in Urban Priority Areas struggle on several counts. First, as we have already seen, there is the difficulty of setting up the necessary networks for recruitment. Second, there are limitations to the lay leadership potential. Third, the potential catechumens may be unused to attending an extended period of instruction, and often there is the problem of teaching the faith in a way which is meaningful to them. However, in spite of such factors, one clergyman in such an area commented: 'It's as good a scheme as any'. It had worked in his parish as well as anything else had!

Some Additional Reflections from a Survey of Small Group Evangelism

Parallel to the development of the catechumenate in the UK has been an interest in gathering people into small (house) groups to provide an introductory experience to the Christian faith. A concept expounded by Michael Wooderson in *Good News Down the Street* (Grove 1982), envisaging usually a six-week course on Christian basics. The six-week unit is complete in itself, but at the end people are invited to join a second group to take things further. The idea has been widely used and modified and many people have become Christians as they have participated in the first unit, a second unit and possibly a third. They have been introduced to Christian worship through the people they met in the groups and, perhaps, finally had found ongoing support for their newly found Christian faith in a regular house group.

Research on small group evangelism in 30 parishes[5] identified some similar trends to the catechumenate. First, the methods of recruitment were almost identical. Second, there were points at which people dropped out, sometimes after a first exploratory meeting, but that is clearly part of the strategy. In many cases people are asked to attend this first meeting with a view to making a choice at the end as to whether they will proceed or not. Third, support for potential new Christians is provided by the Christians who attend the group.

One of the questions on the research paper was: 'What percentage of people attending the basics course continue further?' In churches running courses lasting six weeks or more the average percentage given was over 75 per cent. Three churches said 50 per cent but a significant number of churches gave 80 per cent or more. One contributory factor may be that with a course lasting six sessions or more the new people feel they belong to the group and the group can move on the next stage as a unit.

A further factor which seems to be significant is the opportunity to opt into something else after the current course had ended. As a result of the progression offered, a large number of people eventually find themselves in house groups or fellowship meetings of various kinds. Given the fact that these groups take place within an Anglican structure some naturally join baptism or confirmation classes. Where there is such a follow up structure, this method, like the catechumenate, is a process for leading people to Christian maturity. Further, with the exception of the catechumenal rites, all the essential elements of the catechumenate are present.

There is a further question which needs exploration. Is there any perceivable difference in the kind of people reached by the two methods? Are churches using the catechumenate, for example, more or less successful in persuading those not linked to a church to attend than those using small group evangelism?

The chart below offers a comparison of the number of churches reaching the different categories of people.

	Not linked	outer fringe	inner fringe	regulars
Small groups (30)	7 churches	15 churches	20 churches	19 churches
Catechumenate (12)	8 churches	7 churches	4 churches	10 churches

Less than half of the catechumenate churches provided the kind of detailed information needed to make a comparison. We can therefore only draw provisional conclusions from the samples, but it may suggest that it is easier to persuade outer and inner fringe people to opt into an initial short course, especially if such people have already been baptised or confirmed. It may also be that the catechumenate, because of the baptism/confirmation focus, lends itself better to ministry with people wanting to come to faith for the first time. Further, there is also a certain psychological pressure on clergy to produce confirmees.

However, it must be recognised that the people targeted for small group evangelism vary with practitioners. One church said it aimed to persuade anyone who came through the church door to join a small group i.e. inner and outer fringe people. While another church said that 75 per cent of the people in small groups were not linked with the church. In general, these two illustrations could be paralleled by catechumenal practice. Further detailed work needs to be done in this area.

Notes

1. *The Book of Occasional Offices*, 2nd Edition (The Church Hymnal Corporation, New York 1988)

2. Advent 1991 to May 1992.

3. *Good News Down the Street* (Grove) – a programme for small group evangelism by Michael Wooderson.

4. 'Team Catechumenate'; Clergy Role, Beaconsfield Team Ministry

5. A parallel survey to the one on the catechumenate 1992-1993

Appendix 4

Extract from *The Porvoo Declaration*, proposed as a result of Conversations between The British and Irish Anglican Churches and the Nordic and Baltic Lutheran Churches:

> We, the Church of Denmark, the Church of England, the Estonian Evangelical-Lutheran Church, the Evangelical-Lutheran Church of Finland, the Evangelical-Lutheran Church of Iceland, the Church of Ireland, the Evangelical-Lutheran Church of Latvia, the Evangelical-Lutheran Church of Lithuania, the Church of Norway, the Scottish Episcopal Church, the Church of Sweden and the Church in Wales, on the basis of our common understanding of the nature and purpose of the Church, fundamental agreement in faith and our agreement on episcopacy in the service of the apostolicity of the Church, contained in Chapters II-IV of the *The Porvoo Common Statement*, make the following acknowledgements and commitments:
>
> a   (i) we acknowledge one another's churches as churches belonging to the One, Holy, Catholic and Apostolic Church of Jesus Christ and truly participating in the apostolic mission of the whole people of God; ....
>
> b   we commit ourselves: ...
>
> (iii) to regard baptized members of all our churches as members of our own;....

The declaration leaves open the implications of this for admission to communion. The Bishop of Grimsby, as Anglican co-chairman, explains in his report to Synod, *Communion with the Nordic and Baltic Lutheran Churches* (GS Misc 427) pp.9-10:

Confirmation

> 21. The Porvoo Declaration does not commit the Church of England to dispense with its requirement of episcopal confirmation before someone can be regarded as 'an actual communicant member of the Church of England' for the purpose of holding office, since commitment (iii) deliberately refers specifically to 'baptized members'. However, the members of the Church of England delegation hope that in the future, *after* the approval of the Declaration, the Church of England may be willing to consider legislation to provide that

references to confirmation should be interpreted as meaning either confirmation by a bishop or confirmation by a priest in an episcopally ordered church in communion with the Church of England. This would reflect ancient and medieval practice, and accord with contemporary practice in the Roman Catholic, Orthodox, and episcopal Lutheran Churches, where confirmation by a priest is permissible, in some cases as the norm and in others as an exception. This is a separate issue, which should be discussed on its own merits after the Declaration is approved, since such legislation is not required in order to give effect to the commitments contained in the Declaration, and would go beyond its terms. It is part of a much broader debate, both ecumenically and internationally.

Appendix 5

Canon B.15A OF THE ADMISSION TO HOLY COMMUNION

1. There shall be admitted to the Holy Communion:

   (a) members of the Church of England who have been confirmed in accordance with the rites of that Church or are ready and desirous to be so confirmed or who have been otherwise episcopally confirmed with unction or with the laying on of hands except as provided by the next following Canon;

   (b) baptised persons who are communicant members of other Churches which subscribe to the doctrine of the Holy Trinity, and who are in good standing in their own Church;

   (c) any other baptised persons authorised to be admitted under regulations of the General Synod; and

   (d) any baptised person in immediate danger of death.

2. If any person by virtue of sub-paragraph (b) above receive the Holy Communion over a long period which appears likely to continue indefinitely, the minister shall set before him the normal requirements of the Church of England for communicant status in that Church.

3 Where a minister is in doubt as to the application of this Canon, he shall refer the matter to the bishop of the diocese or other Ordinary and follow his guidance thereon.

Appendix 6

ONE STORY – TWO ENDINGS

Nigel and Rose are both teachers, recent college graduates and members of St Whatnot's church in a slightly run-down (but not desperate) area of town. Both are committed Christians and have joined the church fresh from their experience of college Christian Unions. The vicar, who is very pleased to have them, invites Nigel and Rose to run an evangelism nurture group. He's under pressure so there isn't much time to plan and prepare. Nigel and Rose are left to choose their own material and are simply given a list of 'likely' people.

The couple send typed invitations to twenty people on the list, inviting them to come to the first meeting at their flat at 8 p.m. in three weeks' time. On the relevant evening they put out twenty chairs, provide a light supper for twenty and are a little bit embarrassed when only five people turn up. Nigel opens the group in prayer and asks people to say who they are and why they have come. Rose plays the guitar and there is a half-hearted attempt to sing. Then everyone is asked to turn to Luke 15.11 in their Bible and to read aloud, in turn, a few verses from the passage. Nigel throws in a few questions for the group to discuss.

Some have painfully obvious answers ('What did the younger son do when his money ran out?'). Some are a bit obscure ('What does the famine in the land tell us about the economic climate today?') Nigel and Rose smile a lot but there are awkward silences. It was never like this at the college C.U. Then they show part of the video with several famous Christian speakers who talk about the Christian life. Rose ends the meeting by leading a time of prayer in which Rose prays aloud, then Nigel, then Nigel again, then Rose. Coffee is served and people leave around ten. There is no contact with the group midweek. Only two people return the following Wednesday. Shortly afterwards the group dies.

Dorothy, in her mid-fifties, was quite pleased to receive an invitation to the new group. She was widowed recently and had started coming to church. It took her a while to work out what it was all about. She'd never heard of a 'basics group' and had no idea what it did. The only typed letters she normally received were from her bank manager. She was very lonely, though, and decided to give it a try. Perhaps this was the way to make friends. She asked the vicar for directions to the flat. He seemed pleased she was going and introduced her to Rose, who was very nice but a bit young.

Dorothy left home very early to walk to the group meeting, frightened of being late. She had a fifteen minute walk (it was still daylight, just). She arrived twenty minutes early and spent time looking in shop windows, resisting the temptation to bolt for home. Operating the entry phone to the flats was hard, so was knocking on Nigel and Rose's front door. When Dorothy saw all the chairs it was a relief to know that a lot of people were coming. As the minutes ticked by the chairs became more and more of an embarrassment. There was some attempt at conversation but not much. Dorothy felt awkward and began to wish she hadn't come. The flat was the poshest she'd ever seen; full of paintings and lined with books. All these people here must be very clever ...

Dorothy found it hard to make friends but had just begun to talk to a nice lady on her left when Nigel interrupted and said a prayer. They passed round a kind of hymn book next and the lady got out her guitar. 'That's nice.' thought Dorothy, 'She's going to sing ... Oh my word, they want us all to join in.'

Worse was to follow. Everyone was asked to turn to Luke 15 in their Bibles. Dorothy had to own up to not having a Bible (she was given one). She had no idea where (or what) Luke's gospel was and got in a flummox with the pages. Then everyone was asked to read aloud. Dorothy hadn't read anything aloud since her children were small. Her cheeks burned as she stammered out a few verses. She wished the ground would swallow her up when she made a small mistake.

The rest of the evening didn't mean very much. All Dorothy wanted to do was to get home. They showed a telly programme with a few vicars on that she'd never seen before. They seemed a lot posher than the vicar at the church. She left around ten for her fifteen-minute walk home in the dark. She arrived home trembling and upset, determined never to go to anything like that again. When she didn't appear at church over the next few weeks the vicar assumed that Nigel and Rose were in touch with her. They thought he would go. Neither had time to check and Dorothy was alone in her sorrow.

Nigel and Rose have offered to lead a new evangelism nurture group in the church. They are very gifted but are out of tune with most people in the area. The vicar accepts their offer but he asks another couple, Richard and Anne, to co-lead with them. Richard and Anne are local people and have both become Christians recently, after they brought their daughter to be baptised. They were part of the adult confirmation group a year ago.

The two couples meet the vicar over three evenings and plan the course in great detail. They agree that Nigel and Rose should lead the meetings but that the group will meet at Richard and Anne's house: people will feel more comfortable there. The vicar gives the four leaders a list and the team work hard in the six weeks before the group begins visiting each person on their own territory. Care is taken to explain to each person what the group will be like and to take away their fears. Nigel and Rose, Richard and Anne continue to meet to pray about the course and to plan.

The first evening arrives. There are about ten chairs in the living room, with some more in the kitchen just in case. About ten to eight the doorbell starts ringing and people arrive. It's all a bit hectic for a few minutes. Richard and Rose have gone off in their cars to give lifts to a couple of people hesitant about coming out at night, and Anne is still putting her daughter to bed. There is some nervousness as people are introduced but general amazement as the room begins to fill up and fifteen people are packed in.

Nigel begins the evening by welcoming everyone and suggesting everyone takes a couple of minutes to talk to their neighbour about who they are and why they've come. There's no shortage of things to say. Everyone takes it in turns to introduce their partner to the group. After that people are far more relaxed. Nigel gives some input. Richard and Anne tell the story of how they became Christians. There is some more discussion in groups and a time to ask questions. In no time it's half past nine. Nigel and Richard make the coffee and pass round the biscuits. Nobody seems to want to go home. Transport is arranged for those without cars, both for a lift home and for next week, so no one has to walk. Nigel and Rose liaise with Richard and Anne after the meeting to review what has happened. During the week they arrange to contact each member of the group to check everything was O.K. and also to contact the five who didn't come. The group is under way...

Dorothy is surprised, but pleased, when Anne and Rose call round to invite her to the new group starting in Anne's house. Dorothy has known Richard and Anne by sight for years. She's hesitant about going at first (it's not easy meeting strangers) but going to church has been the only good thing to happen to her since Stan died and it would be good to get to know people better. She decides to make the effort and is relieved to know that Richard will pick her up in the car at 7.45.

Even so, Dorothy is nervous and ready in good time. It's much easier arriving with someone else. Richard and Anne's house is very nice, like hers when she was younger. There are one or two familiar faces there from church and everyone is soon chatting. Dorothy finds herself next to Sue, a young mum. During the opening exercise she finds herself telling Sue all about Stan and his last illness, and all the things that have happened. It's a relief to talk. It seems a bit nerve-racking to have to introduce Sue to the group but everyone else is nervous too. Most people are just like her: wanting to get more involved; wanting to learn more, but nervous at the same time. Richard and Anne's story is really interesting. Fancy a plumber becoming a Christian! Everything that's said makes her think. There's no shortage of things to ask or talk about and Dorothy is quite reluctant to leave at ten o'clock. She arrives home feeling a lot lighter than when she went: like a burden has been lifted.

Anne pops in a few days later just to see how Dorothy got on, which is nice. It's a chance to talk through things Dorothy didn't understand and to ask Anne some questions she didn't dare ask on the night. Dorothy was afraid since the meeting that she was too quiet but Anne is able to reassure her on this. They agree to see each other on Sunday at church and Dorothy finds herself looking forward to each of the group meetings as they come round.

[From *Growing New Christians,* Steve Croft, Marshall Pickering 1993 pp. 84-89.]